iPhone SE
2020

The Complete Beginners Guide to Master the New
iPhone SE (2020) with Tips and Tricks

Alex Leon

Copyright

This book is copyrighted, and no part of this publication may be reproduced or transmitted through any means, be it mechanical, electronic, internet, or otherwise without the permission of the publisher except in a brief quotation or review of the book.

The information in this book is believed to be valid at the date of publication. However, neither the author nor the publisher is legally responsible for any errors or omissions that may be made. The publisher makes no warranty, express or implied, concerning the information contained herein.

ISBN:
USA|UK|Canada
Tech Publishing House

Printed in the United States of America
(c) 2020 by Alex Leon

Table of Contents

CHAPTER ONE

Introduction

The iPhone SE 2020 or iPhone SE 2 is an Apple device that is part of the 13th generation of the iPhones together with the iPhone 11, 11pro, and 11max models. Initially, the iPhone SE model was a low budget 4-inch iPhone before Apple decided to put a pause on the production in 2018. On the 15th of April 2020, it was re-launched, and it replaced the iPhone 8 series.

However, the iPhone SE 2020 comes with a new 4.7-inch model resembling the iPhone 8, while some of the internal hardware components bear similarities to the iPhone 11. The iPhone SE 2020 became the successor to the smaller and lighter previously made iPhone SE 1. Pre-orders of the device began on the 17th of April, 2020, and released eventually on the 24th of April, 2020. Its starting price was at $399 cost for a model with 64GB of storage and, therefore, still a budget phone.

Other iPhones launched previously, like the iPhone 8, iPhone 7, iPhone 6S, or iPhone 6 all have basic shapes just like the 2020 iPhone SE; a 4.7-inch screen with huge bezels atop and below it, a circular home bottom (synonymous to most iPhones) on the bottom with a fingerprint sensor embedded in it.

Like iPhone 7 and 8, the home button is not a physical button that gives a tactile tap back effect when you press on it. Apple has had this design since 2014 and still uses the same design without significant modifications.

An iPhone SE 2020 comes in a standard box containing the following.

- Lightning headphones (EarPods),
- A lightning cable,
- A 5W charger (this iPhone supports fast-charging, but this included charger is not for fast charging),
- Apple stickers,
- User manual and Warranty information,
- A SIM ejector tool.

The iPhone SE 2020 design

The iPhone SE has an aluminum frame with glass at both front and back. The exterior design on the SE 2020 is identical to that of the iPhone 8, except for a centered Apple logo (placement) and absence of an actual iPhone branding. The iPhone SE is available in three colors- black, white, product red edition.

Colors

Meanwhile, the available colors line up with those available in iPhone 8; - silver, space gray, and product (red); iPhone SE uses a deeper shade of black, a brighter shade of white, and a lighter shade of red. In line with the color schemes of iPhone 11series and later iPhones, iPhone SE 2020 features black bezels around the display on all models. The iPhone SE is among the smallest mainstream in-production smartphones launched at that time, with only a screen diagonal of 4.7-inches. Still, it is 30% larger than the first model whose screen diagonal is 4-inch.

Water and Dust Resistance

The iPhone SE 2020 has IP67 water and dust resistance rating; this simply means that it can withstand one meter of water for a maximum of 30minutes and is entirely dustproof. It can hold up water splashes, rain, and brief accidental exposure to water; however, one should avoid intentionally exposing it to water. It is important to note that Apple's warranty does not cover any form of water damage.

Dimension

By dimensions, the iPhone SE 2020, measures 138.4mm in length, 67.3mm in width, 7.3 in thickness, and 5.22 ounces in weight.

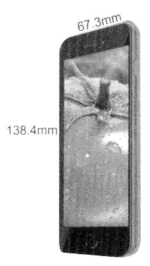

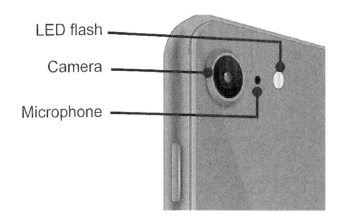

LED flash

Camera

Microphone

Body features

On the back of the iPhone SE 2020 are a single-lens rear camera, a microphone, and an LED flash.

Mute

Volume { Up, Down

Power

On the left side is the power button. On the right is are the mute switch and volume buttons (up and down).

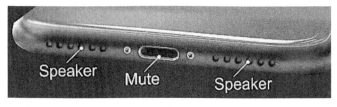

Speaker   Mute   Speaker

At the bottom of the iPhone, is a lightning port and speaker holes. Like the previously launched iPhones, there is no iPhone headphone jack on the iPhone SE 2020; therefore, the need for a Bluetooth or lightning headphones.

Already, the iPhone SE 2020 comes with a lightning headphone, to go wireless, get an AirPod, or other third-party Bluetooth earphones from Amazon.com.

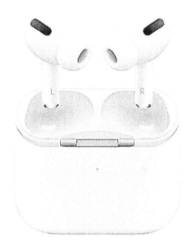

Touch ID

This device also features a Touch fingerprint sensor. The Touch ID Home button coated with a durable sapphire crystal protects the Touch ID sensor and a steel ring for detecting fingerprints.

Typical uses of Touch ID include;

⟩ Unlocking the iPhone

⟩ Filling in passwords with the iCloud Keychain

⟩ Confirming purchases

⟩ Launching passcode-protected apps,

⟩ Validating Apple pay transactions and so on.

Display

For Display features, the iPhone SE has 4.7-inch IPS LCD, the same display size as the iPhone 8 coupled with 1334 by 750 resolution, 326 pixels per inch, and a contrast ratio of 1400:1.

Other display features include;

⟩ Multi-touch capabilities

⟩ True-to-life colors

⟩ P3 wide color support for luxurious color enhancements

⟩ 625 nits max brightness.

True Tone

The iPhone SE 2020 true tone makes use of an ambient light sensor to detect lighting around its environment. Truetone adjusts the color temperature and light intensity to match the screen light for a more natural, comfortable viewing experience and, in turn, ease the strain on eyes when viewing. The iPhone SE 2020 has 4.7 in 120mm True Tone Retina HD display and the IPS technology

Haptic Touch

Haptic Touch is very similar to a 3D-touch, which is available on iPhone 8. It offers the same features but not pressure-sensitive and also does not support multiple functions for every single command. It is best suited for long press or press and holds gestures with haptic feedback. The iPhone SE offers same Haptic Touch features as the iPhone 11, iPhone 11 Pro, iPhone 11 Pro Max

Functions of Haptic Touch

〉 For accessing Quick Actions on the Home screen

〉 For previewing links from Safari

〉 For activating the flashlight on the lock screen

〉 For accessing features in the control center

〉 For expanding notification options

〉 For quick reply options in messages

〉 For deleting undesired apps and so on

A13 Bionic

The iPhone SE is equipped with the A13 Bionic chip, which is the fastest in smartphones, including a pair of machine learning accelerators that allow the CPU run multiple times faster, thereby delivering more than one trillion operations per second. It is way faster than the A11 on iPhone 8. This chip is the same as in the iPhone 11series; it is more power-efficient and improves the battery more than the

A11. In the A13 chip, there is an 8-core Neural Engine that provides faster real-time photo and video analysis. This neural engine powers some significant features like the camera system, and Touch ID

Augmented reality apps

A13 Bionic pairs with iOS 13 to enable new applications that use machine learning and Core ML. The A13 is what also allows extended battery life. The iPhone SE is wireless charging equipped together with QI-certified chargers giving up to 30 minutes charge of 50%. The speed of download is also super-fast with Wi-Fi 6 and Gigabit-class LTE.

Storage Space

The iPhone SE is available in various storage options, which include 64GB, 128GB, and 256GB. The following vary in prices as well

RAM

The iPhone SE 2020 has a 3GB RAM.

Cameras

Because the iPhone SE 2020 is a budget phone, it features just one 12-megapixel, single-lens rear camera. However, it possesses some technology from the iPhone 11 series, which means this device offers better pictures than one can get with iPhone 8. This better picture quality links to the presence of the A13 chip. The camera here is the best single-camera system produced yet. Seeing that it has a wide-angled feature with f/1.8 aperture added with optical image stabilization, a great color capture action, and the next generation Smart HDR for improved highlights and shadow details. It gives a more natural-looking photo. It does not support night mode; meanwhile, despite having just one camera, it supports portrait mode, portrait lighting, and depth control.

In video making, the iPhone SE shoots 4K video at up to 60 frames in seconds; therefore, with 24 and 30 frames, 1080 and 720p shooting modes also available options. Extended dynamic range support is available for a video to 30 frames per second, and optical image stabilization equally possible. Other features available are; the QuickTake video, slo-mo, Autofocus, IR filter, Burst mode, and time-lapse with stabilization. For the front camera, a 7-megapixel front-facing camera has an f/2.2 aperture. It has portrait mode and Depth Control support.

Other features available in the front camera are

- ⟩ Wide color capture
- ⟩ Retina flash
- ⟩ Auto image stabilization
- ⟩ Burst mode
- ⟩ Auto HDR and so on

Battery Life

The battery capacity of the iPhone se2020 is 1,821 mAh, which is the same as that of iphone8. This battery lasts up to 13hours of video playback, 8hours of online video streaming, 40hours of audio playback, and 48hours idle time. This device supports fast charging, which requires a USB-C power adapter that gives at least 18 watts, which also includes 29/30 watts adapters from Apple retail outlets at $49-$50. This UBC-C power adapter and the USB-C lightning cable for fast charging do not come in the pack when you buy the phone; therefore must be purchased separately. What you get with the phone is a USB-A lightning cable and a 5W power adapter. The iPhone SE 2020 possesses in-built wireless charging coil within the glass body to enable wireless charging, which is compatible with any 5W or 7.5W Qi-based wireless charging accessory.

Connectivity

The iPhone SE 2020 supports dual-SIM, wide-ranged Bluetooth, GSM, EDGE, UMTS, HSPA+, DC-HSDPA, CDMA EV-DO, FDD-LTE, TD-LTE, Wi-Fi, NFC, Voice over LTE (VoLTE), Wi-Fi calling, and GPS/GNSS services.

⟩ Dual-SIM
Dual-SIM Support enables users to use two phone numbers at the same time. This

feature is available through the addition of one physical Nano-SIM slot and an eSIM.

⟩ Bluetooth and Wi-Fi

The iPhone SE supports Bluetooth 5.0. This Bluetooth capacity offers a more extended range, faster speeds, tremendous broadcast message ability, and improved sharing of data with other wireless technologies compared to Bluetooth 4.2. The iPhone SE 2020 also supports Wi-Fi 6 which is the latest Wi-Fi protocol and downloads about 38percent faster than Wi-Fi 5

⟩ Gigabit LTE

Like the iPhone 11, the iPhone SE enables Gigabit-class LTE with 2x2 MIMO and LAA, enabling the same LTE bands just like the iPhone 11. These bands are;1,2,3,4,5,6,7, 8, 12, 13,14,17,18,19,20,25,26,29,30,66 with the FDD-LTE bands and 34,38,39,40,41,42,46, and 48 TD-LTE bands.

⟩ GPS and NFC

The iPhone SE supports GPS, GLONASS, Galileo, and QZSS location services. NFC with reader mode is available; there is also a background tag feature that allows this device to scan NFC tags without opening it first. It also supports Express Cards with power reserve; this means it can be used as a transit card for public transits and function even when the device is off.

Other features of the iPhone SE 2020 are;
- ⟩ Hearing aid compatibility with the M3, T4.
- ⟩ For sound, it has stereo speakers.
- ⟩ Graphics processing unit (GPU) in iPhone SE 2020 is the Apple-designed quad-core
- ⟩ The central processing unit (CPU) of iPhone SE 2 is a Hexa-core twice high lightning cores at 2.65 GHz and a low-power Thunder cores 1.82 GHz.

iPhone SE (2020) vs. iPhone 8 differences summary

- iPhone SE comes with an Apple A13 Bionic chip vs. Apple A11 Bionic chip on the iPhone 8
- Only iPhone SE has support for Portrait mode

- Only iPhone SE has extended dynamic range for video at 30fps, stereo sound recording
- Only iPhone SE has features the Next-generation Smart-HDR for photos
- iPhone SE has a starting price of $400 vs. $450 starting price for the iPhone 8
- No Plus-sized model on the iPhone SE
- No 3D Touch on iPhone SE, it only supports Haptic Touch) vs. on iPhone 8 which support 3D Touch
- Dual SIM card support on the iPhone SE (which includes a nanoSIM + eSIM) vs. single SIM for iPhone 8
- The iPhone SE has faster connectivity for cellular, Wi-Fi with Wi-Fi 6 support)

CHAPTER TWO

Getting Started with the iPhone SE 2020

To unbox, take off the wrappers and remove the box tops. Unbox the top paper to reveal its content. In there is a welcome to the iPhone SE document that gives a little overview of the iPhone, a SIM card removal tool, and two iPhone stickers as well as a warranty card. However, if it is a red product that was purchased, there will be a little red pamphlet also. Each time a customer buys a red product, a portion of the money goes to fight HIV/AIDS, or any current issue faced.

How to insert the SIM Card

To insert a SIM card, use the SIM card ejector tool into the tiny hole on the SIM card tray to pop it out. Then place the SIM card on the tray and push it back in.

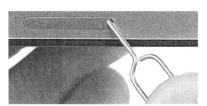 

Turning On the iPhone SE 2020 for the first time

To turn on the phone, long-press the power button till the Apple logo comes on.

Setting up the iPhone SE 2020

Once the iPhone is powered on for the first time, after the Apple logo must have appeared, the next screen will display a *Hello* message.

⟩ Press the home button to start the setup process.

⟩ Select your preferred language

⟩ Select your region

⟩ The next screen shows the *QuickStart* option

The QuickStart Setup

To 'Quick Start' the setup, bring your previous phone close to the new phone and ensure both phone batteries are fully charged. Turn on Bluetooth on both phones, and then use your former iPhone camera to scan the QR code displayed on your new iPhone.

The iPhone SE will then requests a passcode from the previous phone, after which it presents a page that shows setting up the phone.

Next is to set up Touch ID; do this by tapping on the home button multiple times as requested by the phone. When this is complete, click *'Continue.'*

Next is to either transfer information to your old phone, from iCloud, or go to *other options* and set it up as new. You can now restore apps and data or just ignore them.

Depending on the GB variance, it will either display Settings From Other or Terms & Conditions pages and then continue with the settings based on preferences. Down along the setup process after selecting your preference, is the Home button haptic feedback setting for your home button.

CHAPTER THREE

Basic Task and Settings

When it comes to carrying out settings on the iPhone SE 2020, the settings app icon on the Home screen is where to tap on to gain access.

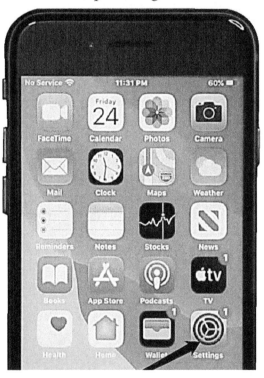

Most of the modifications to be carried out on the iPhone SE require using the settings app with a gear icon. We will be using the settings app to complete most tasks in this guide.

Charging the Battery

The iPhone SE 2020 comes with an internal Lithium-ion rechargeable battery; therefore, to charge this phone, use the lighting-to-USB cable after in the box. When using a power outlet, connect the lightning-to-USB cable to the iPhone and plug it into the power adaptor. Then plug the power adaptor to the power outlet.

When using a power bank, plug the lightning cable directly to the USB port on the power bank after connecting the cable to the iPhone.

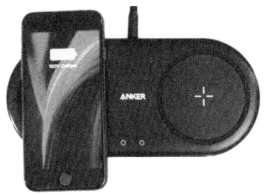

To use the wireless charging option, use any compatible wireless charger by placing the back of the iPhone on the panel. Fast-charging is attainable with an 18watt or any higher adapter, and in 30 minutes, charges up to 50% of its battery power.

Checking the Battery Capacity

Checking the battery capacity of the new iPhone SE 2020 is one of the vital inspections to be carried out immediately after purchase.

To check the iPhone battery capacity, tap on the Settings app, and then scroll down and select *Battery*.

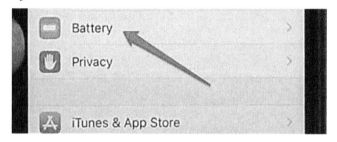

On the next screen, tap on Battery Health. What should display as the battery capacity should be 100% to 999%, indicating the battery is brand new.

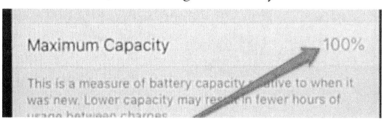

If the battery capacity is below 98%, it is wise to have the iPhone replaced.

Turning on the Battery Percentage Indicator

The battery percentage indicator gives visual information about the battery status numerically.

To turn on the battery percentage display, tap on the Settings app, and then scroll down and select Battery.

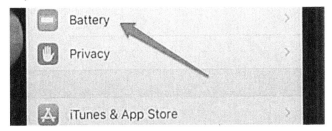

On the next screen, toggle on Battery Percentage to complete the process.

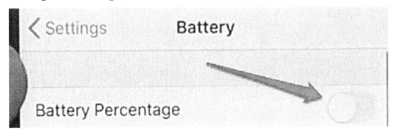

Change the Auto-lock Settings

The Auto-lock feature on the iPhone SE 2020 is both a security and battery life extension settings. When the iPhone is ideal, it automatically turns off the display to save battery or prevent someone else from accidentally using the iPhone.

By default, the Auto-lock setting is at 4 minutes. It can be as low as 30 seconds. To turn on the Auto-Lock or modify the settings, tap on the Settings app, and then scroll down and go into Display & Brightness.

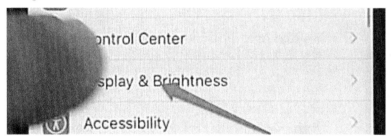

Next, scroll down and tap on Auto-Lock.

Ensure it is not kept on Never. Change the timing to 30 seconds to get an optimal result.

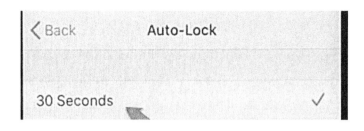

Turn on Bold Text

This setting allows the text to look bold for easy viewing. Most times, when using the iPhone under bright direct sunlight, it might be challenging to read the text on the screen. Turning on the Bold Text settings make the reading of text more comfortable on the iPhone.

To turn on this feature, tap on the Settings app, and then scroll down and go into Display & Brightness.

Next, toggle on the Bold Text settings.

Turn off Automatic Brightness

The iPhone SE will keep dimming because Auto-Brightness enabled. The auto-brightness feature makes the iPhone SE display to be too low in brightness or too bright based on ambient lighting of the surrounding. Turn off Auto-Brightness if the iPhone keeps dimming to stop. Tap on the Settings and go into Accessibility. Next, tap on the Display & Text Size option.

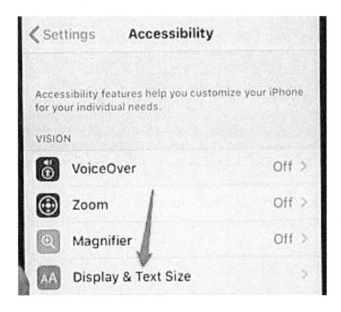

Scroll down and toggle off the Auto-Brightness feature.

Turn off Notification and Control Center access when iPhone is Locked

Take control of privacy by hiding sensitive content and options whenever the iPhone is locked.

When the iPhone is locked and still displaying notifications, when the power button used, it will be safer for security reasons to hide these notifications. To do this on the iPhone, go to the Settings app and scroll down to *Touch ID and Passcode*, then enter the iPhone passcode to have access to make the changes. Next, scroll to *Allow Access When Locked* tab and disable all the features enabled.

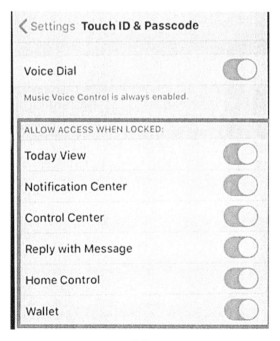

Enable Touch ID for use in iPhone Unlock, iTunes, Apple Pay, and Password AutoFill

When this setting is enabled, you can use your Touch ID to unlock your iPhone, access the app store, confirm an online payment with Apple Pay, and autoFill your password.

To do this on the iPhone, go to the Settings app and scroll down to *Touch ID and Passcode*, then enter your Passcode, and on the next screen, toggle ON the features.

Register more Fingerprints to TouchID

Once done, adding a fingerprint to the iPhone SE 2020, the setup process can continue. Meanwhile, the iPhone can still accommodate up to five fingerprints to the Touch ID. This way, some family members can have their fingerprints registered to have access to the iPhone SE.

Go to the Settings app and scroll down to "Touch ID & Passcode." Next, enter the passcode manually to proceed.

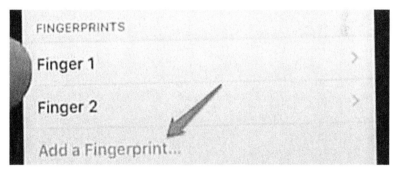

You will see a list of fingerprints already registered; "Finger 1" happens to be the fingerprint registered during the iPhone setup. To add a fingerprint, tap on the *Add a Fingerprint* button and complete the process.

Turn on Raise to Wake Feature

When a user picks up the iPhone SE 2020 to look at the screen, it awakens the Lock screen automatically. You can quickly check your notifications if enabled, access your iPhone Control Centre, swipe left to take a quick photo, or swipe right to access your widgets.

Go to the Settings app and scroll down to "Display & Brightness." Next, scroll down to *Raise to Wake* option and toggle it On.

Hide and Disable Apps from other Users

Should much download of apps be done on the iPhone SE, the icons for each of these apps will clutter the home screen. To keep apps private from other users, the iOS 13 on the iPhone SE allows hiding of apps.

Go to the Settings app and scroll down to *Screen Time* option and select the *Content & Privacy Restrictions* option.

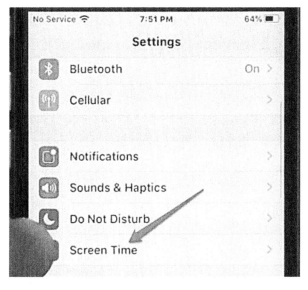

Enter the iPhone passcode, select apps to allow and disable apps to hide from the iPhone.

CHAPTER FOUR

Taking Photos and Recording Videos

The iPhone SE 2020 comes with both a single rear and front camera. With the rear camera equipped with 12MP and features like True Tone flash with Slow Sync, Optical image stabilization (OIS), portrait mode with advanced Bokeh and Depth Control, Portrait Lighting, and also a next-generation Smart HDR for photos. Aside from that it can record 4K video at 24, 30, or 60fps with OIS and stereo recording for video.

The front camera, however, features an upgraded 7MP sensor with an f/2.2 aperture, Auto HDR for photos, portrait lighting, and portrait mode. It also records a 1080 HD video at 30fps.

Best accessories for taking photographs on iPhone SE 2020

While the iPhone SE 2020 already has impressive features to enhance your photographs, a wide range of accessories are available to improve your photography experience and take it to the next level.

Tripod

A tripod is one of the essential accessories that can be own by a photographer, either mobile or otherwise. It is necessary for long exposures and self-portraits.

To choose the best iPhone tripod, make the selection based on preference. For example, to maintain the free feel in photography, consider a smaller, lightweight, conveniently available tripod. These small, extremely compact, flexible, and highly useful tripods come in various models available online and in tech shops. Grip tight Gorrilapods and lollipop tripods are good options.

The mounts hold the iPhone SE steady and secure via an integrated pin-joint mount. The folding legs make it extremely portable and easy to carry in a pocket, handbag, backpack, or camera bag

Remote Shutter Release

Though the iPhone SE camera's self-timer is convenient, using a remote shutter release will give more control when taking shots. The most comfortable remote shutter release comes with the iPhone box.

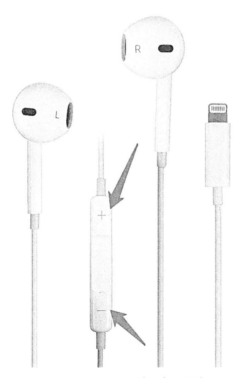

The earpods that came with the iPhone SE have an in-built button that controls the phone's volume. However, many camera apps allow the use of iPhone volume buttons to control the shutter release, meaning you can use the volume controls on the earbud in the same manner. For self-portraits, a better option is a wireless shutter release such as Muku Shutter. This device connects over Bluetooth to control shutter release.

External Battery/Charger

It is always prudent to carry a plug-in charger, recharging the iPhone even when away from home is necessary. However, if no access to AC power for recharging the iPhone, it will be convenient to carry along a DC power option.

Fortunately, just like most tripods, there are many options open to users based on their specific needs and budget. The most affordable and most uncomplicated external batteries will charge the iPhone SE 1-2 times. The best feature of these batteries/chargers is their size and can easily fit into a pocket. However, larger chargers will require a backpack/bag. These larger ones can charge the iPhone SE up to 7times, and perfect for photo-shooting excursions or camping.

External Lenses

To also improve picture quality, wide-angle, and other amazing features is to use add-on lenses.

One of the best ways to bridge the gap between mobile photography and DSLR is the use of these available add-on lenses. They are compact, easy to attach, and give an outstanding outcome. The best option to start with is the 4-in-1 lens combo. It is classic and easy to use.

External Light Source

Although the iPhone SE 2020 has a built-in flashlight that can work correctly, it still does not have the 'night mode' feature, and in low-light situations, it becomes an issue. An external light source will provide better light quality, but it also enhances the iPhone photography. Aside from this, the portable light source can also adjust the angle of the light source, modify the power levels to control light strength, and evenly distribute it.

Mobile Wireless Storage Drives

For long term video or photo shooting, consider carrying an external storage device along. These external storage devices are typically flash-based memory drives that can upload files to free up memory on the iPhone. Uploading data to a cloud-based storage service such as iCloud Photos, Dropbox, or Google Drive is an option. Nevertheless, there has to be access to a high-speed Wi-Fi connection or a considerable data plan with a cellular service provider.

For immediate backup of photos while still shooting or busy, then an external storage device is the best option.

Camera bag

A camera bag may seem unnecessary but required to carry these gadgets. Using a backpack is also a good option. To access all devices and travel as light as possible, then a camera bag will be the best option.

How to take a photo on iPhone SE 2020

From the home screen tap the camera app, it will traditionally open up with the Photo mode selected.

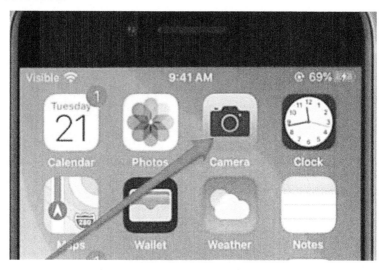

Swipe left or right to choose modes such as Pano, Portrait, Video, and so on.

Then tap the shutter button or either of the volume buttons to take a shot.

The preview appears at the bottom left. When you tap on it, you have several options to either 'Share,' like the 'Photo,' 'Edit,' the photo with several other editing features, or delete.

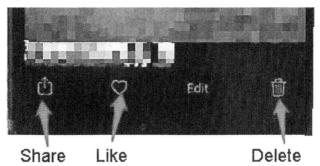

Share   Like   Delete

Also, to focus on a particular subject, just tap on the preferred subject and tap on the shutter button to take the photo. If, after focusing on a subject, you move the phone, you will lose the focus. However, to lock the focus in, hold your finger down on the subject to lock it in.

After that, you would see the 'AE/AF Lock' at the top then tap the shutter button to take the photo. To remove the locked focus, just tap on the screen. Alternatively, you can simply pull up the control center and tap on the camera icon.

To the upper left of the camera app screen is a lightning icon, which is the flash.

You can turn it on or off;

however, by default, it is in auto mode; this means the iPhone decides when it's best to use it.

To access more settings, swipe up the screen.

Other settings include the size, which is the aspect ratio with 4:3 as default, timer, and live filters. Tap on the circle with an arrow at the center to display these settings.

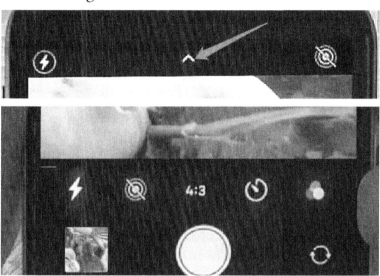

At the bottom right is kind of circle with arrow ends, tap to flip between the rear camera and the front-facing camera.

With the front camera, a user will be able to use most of the rear camera features to modify shot.

How to use portrait mode on iPhone SE cameras

Portrait mode creates a depth-of-field effect and allows you to compose a photo that keeps the subject sharply clear while blurring the background. You can add lighting effects to photos and also take a selfie with the portrait mode. You can also modify how much or how little you want the blur effect to be, and it works best with the rear-facing camera. You can get Natural light, Studio Couture, Stage, Stage light mono, and high key light mono along with these. Utilize it, just tap on it, and drag it across to take a photo with any of the options you want.

To take a photo in portrait mode, start the Camera app, and swipe to portrait mode, then follow the on screen tips.

When in portrait mode, the lighting effect name, such as Natural Light turns yellow. Tap the shutter button to take a shot.

The camera notifies you when you are too close or too far away, or if your environment is darker. You can also use True Tone flash, Set a Timer, and even Apply Filters.

After taking a photo, you can use the built-in editing features to take actions like Crop and Auto-Enhance.

To zoom and use a Wide camera, tap the 2x button. To add portrait lighting, open the Photo app, and select Portrait mode photo, you wish to change and tap Edit. The lighting effect appears in the bottom part of the photo. Swipe the lighting effect to choose the one you want and tap Done.

How to take a selfie in portrait mode

1. Open the camera app,
2. Swipe to portrait mode,
3. Tap the front-rear camera switching button
4. Take your selfie with either of the volume buttons.

How to adjust depth control and portrait lighting on selfies in portrait mode

1. Tap a portrait mode photo in your photo library
2. Tap Edit and then tap the Depth Control button or Portrait Lighting button to adjust portrait lighting. A slider appears below the photo.

Drag the slider to the left or right to modify the effect and tap Done.

How to take live photos on iPhone SE 2020

Open the camera app and make sure your Camera is in Live Mode and turn on Live Photos.

Hold your device still and tap the shutter button. Live Photos feature is always on; however, you can turn it off temporarily or permanently.

How to find and play live photos on iPhone SE 2020

Open the photos app and tap the Albums tab and Scroll down to mafia types and then tap Live photo. To change the key photo, open the live photo and tap Edit. Tap the live photo button and move the slider to and fro to change the frame

Release your finger and then tap Make Key Photo, tap Done.

The key photo is the main one that appears when you view the photo.

How to Edit Live Photos

To edit Live photos, open the Photos app and tap the Photos tab, select the live photo you wish to edit, Tap Edit and then make your adjustments based on preference when you finish tap Done.

How to Share live Photos

Open the photo you want to share and tap the share button, however, if you're going to share as still photo and not live, tap live in the upper left corner and choose how you want to share your photo on your iPhone SE 2.

How to turn off Live Photos

Tap the Live Photos button to turn off live photos, and a slash through the button indicates the feature is off. To keep this feature off permanently, open the Settings app, tap Camera, and tap Preserve Setting, ensure that the switch next to live photos is on.

How to take Panorama Photo on iPhone SE 2020

If you want to take a Panorama Photo, open your Camera app, and swipe along the screen to choose Pano mode.

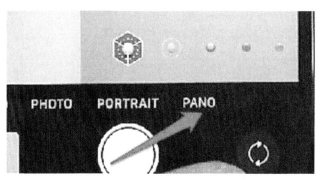

Next, point your camera to your starting point, tap the shutter button, and move across the area you want to snap while keeping your hand stable. Tap Stop when you finish

How to Capture with Timelapse

Start the camera app and swipe across the screen to choose options. Tap on timelapse

Tap the shutter button and leave to record whatever it is you want to record and tap Stop.

How to take Burst shots

You can take Burst shots with both front and rear cameras. To take burst shots, swipe the shutter button to the left to take several-fir photos. The counter displays how many shots you took at a go. Lift your finger to stop.

To select which photos to keep, tap the burst thumbnail and then tap select. Suggested photos to preserve have gray dots below it. To save an individual photo, tap the circle in the lower-right corner of each photo. Then tap done.

How to Adjust the Camera's Focus and Exposure

Although the iPhone SE2 camera automatically sets the focus, exposure, and face detection that balances the exposure across many faces, if you still want to adjust the focus, open the Camera app manually. Tap the screen to show the automatic focus area and exposure setting. Then tap an area to focus there. Next to the focus area, drag the sun-looking icon up and down to adjust the exposure.

How to use the Slow-Motion (Slo-mo)

By default, HD240 is the set pace, but you can change it to 120; however, this is just the speed; 240 will give the slowest option. You can swipe the screen to reveal other options. To take a slo-mo video, open the camera app and swipe left to choose the slo-mo feature. Focus on a subject, tap the shutter button, and make whatever movement you wish to make. When you finish tap Done.

How to use High Dynamic Range (HDR)

iPhone SE 2020 automatically uses HDR for both front and rear cameras when it is most effective. But if you want to turn off automatic HDR or Smart HDR, go to settings and tap camera then turn off Smart HDR. Then from the camera display screen, tap HDR to turn it off or on.

CHAPTER FIVE

Siri on the iPhone SE 2020

Siri Settings

To set up Siri or adjust any of its functions, tap the Settings app from the home screen, choose Siri & search. The features you can adjust include

- Changing Siri's voice
- Stop Siri from responding to the voice command
- Change language
- Adjust Siri voice volume and so on

Funny things to ask Siri

What does Siri mean?

Are you a robot?

Are you intelligent?

Do you follow the three laws of robotics?

What do you dream about?

How old are you?

Can you stop time?

Why do you vibrate?

What are you made off?

What's your favorite color?

What are you scared of?

Do you have any pests?

What are you doing later?

What's your best pick up line?

Will you go out on a date with me?

Did god create you?

What are you wearing?

How to make requests using Siri

To make a request using Siri, say 'Hey Siri' and say what you need or your command. If Siri misunderstands you, correct it by re-phrasing your request. You can also spell out the parts of your request that it couldn't understand. Another method of correcting Siri is editing your request with text.

To permanently use text to communicate with Siri, tap the Settings app from the home screen, select Accessibility, and tap Siri. Then turn on type words to Siri.

How to Turn Off Siri

1: Open the Settings menu.

2: Scroll to the Siri option.

3: Tap the button to the right of Siri at the top of
  the screen and toggle off the button.

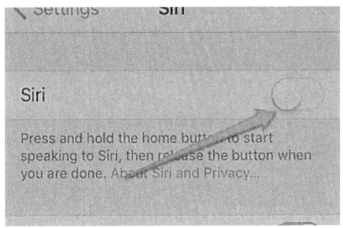

CHAPTER SIX

Using the Safari Browser and Mail
How to surf the web

You must connect your iPhone to a Wi-Fi network directly to an internet provider or a public Wi-F network, otherwise known as a hotspot. Anothe option is the paid data network provided by Verizon, AT&T, or sprint.

To surf the web, use the safari app. This app aid web browsing, and if you used the same Apple IE to sign in iCloud in your other devices, you coulc see all your previous activities on your iPhone. Just tap on the safari app and type in your search key or URL on the search field and tap Go on the keyboard.

How to choose a Search Engine

Tap the Settings app from the home screen, choose Safari and tap Search Engine. If you wish to preview a link without visiting the site, tap and hold it in Safari to preview. To close the preview and remain on your current page, tap anywhere outside the preview window.

How to keep Bookmarks

To bookmark the page currently are, tap and hold the bookmark icon. Then tap on Add bookmark.

To view your bookmarked pages, tap the bookmark icon then tap Bookmarks, however, if you want to create a folder, delete, rename bookmarks, tap Edit.

How to add a Website icon to the Home Screen

From the website, tap the upload icon and then tap the add button to the home screen.

How to Save a Reading list for Later View

Add your current page to the reading list, tap the upload icon, and then tap Add to the reading list.

To view your reading list, tap the book icon and tap the goggle icon the swipe the page left to delete it.

For you not to lose your reading list at any time, save to iCloud. Just below the reading list, tap the Settings app from the home screen, tap Safari, and turn on Automatically Save Offline.

How to Fill Forms

To fill in a form, tap the field to bring up the keyboard and fill in your content.

To fill in contact information in forms automatically, tap Autofill Contact above the keyboard; however, the website has to support AutoFill.

To submit a form, tap GO or the link supplied by the webpage.

How to Disable Annoying Pop-up Adverts

Use reader view to hide pop-up adverts and show only relevant text and images. To hide adverts, tap the double capitalized A (AA) icon at the left end of the address field and tap Show Reader View.

To block pop-up adverts, tap the Settings app from the home screen, select Safari and turn on Block Pop-ups.

How to Write Mail

Ask Siri by uttering a command like "New email Samson Dove." Alternatively, open the Mail app from the home screen, tap the add icon, and tap in the Mail. Type the message you want to send or save as draft

How to Preview Mail

To preview a mail in the mailbox, tap and hold the Mail to preview it. And also, several options are available like a reply, filing, delete, and so on. However, to extend preview lines, tap the Settings app from the home screen, select Mail, and tap Preview, now select about 3-5 lines.

How to Delete Mails

To delete a mail while viewing it, tap the delete icon at the button of the Mail

To delete while viewing the mail list, simply swipe the Mail to the left, then choose the delete icon from the menu.

To recover a deleted mail, go to the accounts Trash mailbox, the tap to open the Mail.

How to Print a Mail

To print a mail, tap, and hold the Mail, from options, select the Print.

Important Mail settings

Notification settings: From the Settings app, select Notifications, and scroll to select Mail, Tap the switch to allow notifications.

Mail accounts: tap the Settings app from the home screen and scroll down to passwords & Accounts, tap it. Select the Account to manage

To/Cc: tap the Settings app from the home screen, select Mail. Touch the switch next to Show To/Cc Labels to switch it on.

Loading Remote Images: tap the Settings app from the home screen, scroll to select Mail and tap to switch on Load Remote Images.

Signature: open the Settings app from the home screen, scroll to select Mail then tap signature and add your new signature

CHAPTER SEVEN

Music and iTunes

How to use Apple Music on iPhone SE

Use the Apple Music app, tap it from the home screen, and utilize the tabs at the bottom of the screen, which includes; Library, For You, Browse, Radio, and Search.

How to use Siri and Voice Control to play Music

To use Siri and voice control to play music, say "Hey Siri" and tell Siri what you wish to listen to

How to Play Music

To play a song, tap on the Library tab and select a song by scrolling up and tapping on the desired song.

How to add Music

You can download and add songs and Music from Apple music. You can offline stream the songs you add to the iPhone SE. If you want to add songs from Apple Music to Library, long hold a song, album or playlist or when viewing the Music, and tap Add to add them to individual songs.

Important Music Settings

Equalization: open the Settings app from the home screen, select Music and the tap on EQ

Volume: open the Settings app from the home screen, choose Music, and select Volume Limit.

How to search for Music on iTunes

To search for Music on iTunes, use the search bar at the top right corner of the iTunes window and type in the artist, song title, or album to get the Music.

Important iTunes Settings

Automatic downloads: Open the Settings app from the home screen, tap the place where you have you name, select iTunes & App Store, and Below Automatic Downloads, tap to turn it on.

Download only with Wi-Fi: tap the Settings app from the home screen, tap on your name and below cellular data, and tap on Automatic Downloads to turn it off.

CHAPTER EIGHT

Calendar and Photos

How to use Several Calendars on iPhone SE

Use several Calendars on iPhone SE 2, open the Calendar app from the home screen, and select the calendars you wish to use. Add extra features to them. Down the page, tap US Holidays to add national holidays to your calendar or tap Birthdays to add birthdays from your contacts to your calendar.

How to share iCloud Calendars

To share iCloud Calendars, you have to create an iCloud calendar; therefore, touch the calendar at the bottom of the screen, select Add Calendar and, type a name for your newly created calendar. After that, tap Done.

To share iCloud Calendars, touch Calendars at the bottom of your phone screen, tap the info icon next to the iCloud calendar you want to share. To add a recipient, enter the name or email address and tap Add.

Important Calendar Settings

Notifications: open the Settings app from the home screen, select Notification, choose calendars and adjust based on preference

Delete calendar: tap calendars at the bottom of the screen, tap the info icon close to the calendar you want to delete and select delete calendar.

How to View Videos and Photos

Open the Photos app from the home screen and browse photos and videos you want to view using the Photos, For You, Albums, and search tabs.

How to use the iCloud Photo Library

If you want to use iCloud Photos, open the Settings app from the home screen and tap where you have your name, select iCloud, then choose Photos and turn on iCloud Photos.

How to share iCloud Photos

To share iCloud Photos, you have to turn on Shared Albums; from the home screen, select the Settings app, tap on where you have your name, and select iCloud, then choose Photos and turn on Shared Albums.

To create a shared album, tap the add button in the Albums tab and select a new shared album, name the album and tap Next. Now choose the people to invite or use an email address and tap on Create. Every time you need to add photos to your shared album, do this; in the Album tab, choose a shared album and tap the add button, choose what items you want to share, and tap Done.

How to Edit and Crop Photos

If you want to edit photos, there are several tools available on the iPhone SE2 photos app. These tools include

- Light and Color balance,
- Crop, trim and flip pictures,
- Straighten or adjust perspective,
- Filter effects and many more.

To crop a photo, open the photos app from the home screen and tap the photo you want to crop for a full-screen view. Tap Edit, then tap the crop icon and using your finger drag or pinch on the screen to your preferred size.

How to Print Photos Directly from the iPhone SE

To print a photo directly from the iPhone SE 2, open the Photos app from the home screen and open the photo you want to write and tap the share button or icon then tap Print.

How to import Videos and Photos

To import Videos and Photos from an external gadget, put the camera adapter into the lightning connector on the iPhone SE 2. Use the camera USB cable to connect the camera to the camera adapter and turn on the camera. Ensure the camera is in transfer mode now open photos on the iPhone SE 2 and tap import. Choose the photos and videos you want, and the location you are moving them to of just tap import all. When you finish importing the items, disconnect the camera adapter from the iPhone.

Important Photo Settings

Preserve settings: to use the Preserve Setting feature, open the Settings app from the home screen, select camera and tap on Preserve Settings

Enable grid lines: Open the Settings app from the home screen, choose Camera, and tap on the switch close to Grid to turn it on.

CHAPTER NINE

The App Store, iBook, and Health

How to Find Apps

To find apps, ask Siri using a command like "search Appstore for football apps" or open the Appstore app and tap any of the following options; Games o Apps, Today, Arcade, and Search.

How to Purchase and Download Apps

To purchase and download an app on the Appstore first, search the app and tap the price on it however, if the app is free, there will be no price tag therefore, just tap Get.

If you see an iCloud icon on it in place of a price tag, it means you already bought the app, so you now download without a charge.

Important AppStore Settings

Subscriptions: To manage your subscriptions, tap your profile picture located at the top right and tap Subscriptions

Appstore setting: To adjust Appstore settings based on convenience and preference, tap on the Setting app from the home screen, tap where your name is, and choose to

- Automatic downloads
- Auto-app updates
- Use of cellular data
- Video Autoplay

How to get Books

To get books, open the Book app from the home screen, tap Book store, or Audiobooks to browse titles or authors. You can also tap the search to look for a specific title. Select the book you want by tapping the book cover to reveal more details, show a sample, or listen to a sample. To buy the book tap on buy. However, if the book is free, tap Get.

How to Read Books

To read a book with the book app, tap your Library or Reading Now tab, and select the cover of the book you want to read to open it. Swipe left or right to flip pages. To close the book, tap the center of the current page you are reading to reveal controls and tap Back.

How to organize books

To organize your books in the book app, create a collection, and add your books to it. To create a collection, tap Library, tap Collections, and now tap New Collection. Name the collection for easy access. If you need to add a book your collection, tap the three dots below the book cover, and tap Add to Collection.

How to read PDF files on your iPhone SE

To read a PDF document, tap and hold the PDF attachment and tap Copy to Books.

Important iBook Settings

Sort books: to sort books in the Book app, select Library and scroll down, tap any word that appears next to Sort or Sort by after this choose recent, title author or manually to sort your books.

Remove items: to free more space on your iPhone, delete books you don't need. To remove them, tap the Library, tap Edit, then tap the items you may want to remove and tap the Delete button and select Delete.

How to connect your iPhone to Apple Watch

Wear your Apple Watch on your wrist and turn it on using the side button, then bring your iPhone SE 2 close to the Apple Watch and wait for your iPhone to display the pairing screen and tap Continue.

How to collect Health and Fitness Data

When setting up the Health app, they request you enter your health information and set up a health profile. To set this health profile, tap your profile picture located at the top right of the summary screen, tap Health profile, and select Edit. Type in the fields required and tap Done; this is to add your data manually. You can also collect data from other sources like apple watch (heart rate), headphones (audio levels), and other devices.

How to Share health and Fitness data

If you want to Share Health and Fitness data, tag your profile picture at the top right, and select Export, all data, and then select a sharing method. Then tap Send or Done, depending on your sharing method.

How to Create an Emergency Medical ID

To create an emergency medical ID, tap your profile picture at the top right, select Medical ID. Select Get Started, fill in the required field.

CHAPTER TEN

Weather app, Maps and, Clock

How to check the Weather on the Weather App

To check the weather on the Weather app, ensure you switch on locations services. To turn on Location services, open the Settings app from the home screen, select Privacy and tap Location service the switch it on, or simply ask Siri with a command like "how sunny is going to be today."

Check the weather on the weather app, open the weather app from the home screen, and display the day's weather.

How to add Cities to the Weather App

To add a city to the weather app, tap the triple horizontal line at the left-hand side down the screen to view the weather list and touch the add button, type in the city name to add the city.

How to find Places on the Map App

To find places on the map app, open the Map app from the home screen, and tap the search field, type

in the name of the area you want to search and hi
GO on your keyboard. Also, aside from using th
name of the place to explore, you can use th
intersections, areas, landmarks, Zip code:
businesses.

How to Share Location
To share location on the Map app, tap a place o
the Map and tap on the share button/icon on th
information card then select an option to shar
alternatively you can tap and hold the location yo
want to share and select Share location

How to get Direction on the Map App
To get directions on the Map app, touch and hol
the place you need direction to, then tap Direction
or just tap the Location and select Directions fron
the information card.

How to use 3D and Flyover views on th
Maps
To use Flyover views on the Map app, select th
name of the city you want to view

Important Map Settings

Change transportation: to change transportation type, open the Settings app from the home screen, select Apps, select Maps, and choose your preferred mode of transportation (driving, walking, or Transit.)

Compass: to enable compass, open the Settings app from the home screen, select Maps, and choose Driving and Navigation, then tap the switch close to compass to allow for it.

English Map labels: In case you need to use the Map app in a non-English language, open the Settings app, select Maps and tap the switch close to Always in English to disable it.

How to set the Alarm and timers on iPhone SE

To set the Alarm, open the Clock app from the home screen, choose Alarm, and tap the Add icon (+). Set the alarm time and select from the options available. They include; Repeat Snooze, Label, and Sound.

CHAPTER ELEVEN

Advanced Tips and Tricks

Turning on Dark Mode

Swipe up from the bottom of the iPhone to go to the control center.

Next, press and hold on the brightness button and use options below to choose your preference.

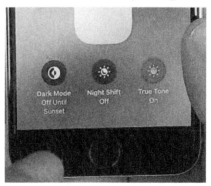

Changing Wallpaper on the iPhone SE 2020

Tap on the Settings app from the Home screen and scroll down to Wallpaper.

Tap on create a new wallpaper to choose between dynamic and stills wallpapers.

Bluetooth connection on the iPhone SE 2020

To use Bluetooth, tap the Settings app from the Home screen, tap Bluetooth, and tap the switch to turn on the feature.

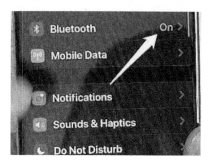

The phone automatically searches for available Bluetooth devices. On the device, you want to connect with, turn on the Bluetooth, and make it discoverable.

Once the iPhone finishes the search, in the list that appears to tap the device (name) you wish to pair your iPhone with, enter the passcode/passkey on the keypad that appears on your phone if it is requested. When you finish, tap 'settings' again, and tap the switch to turn 'off' your Bluetooth and make it undiscoverable.

Wi-Fi connection on iPhone SE 2020

On the device which you want to join the network, tap on Settings, and turn on the Hotspot.

On your iPhone SE 2020 tap on the Settings app and tap Wi-Fi to switch it On.   Under Choose a Network, tap the name of the network you wish to join.

Ensure both devices are close at proximity, or the network you want to join has a strong signals.

Connect the iPhone to the Internet

Select the Settings app from the home screen; tap Mobile Data and select Mobile Data Options, Scroll down to select Reset Settings.

By now the phone will reset to default Internet and MMS settings. However, if you are still unable to access the Internet, follow these instructions

>) Make sure Wi-Fi is off
>) Tap mobile data, select mobile data options and tap mobile data networks.
>) Enter internet information manually, and this will set it up manually and should work

Restore backed up files from iTunes to iPhone SE 2020

To restore backed up files, open iTunes, connect your iPhone to a computer and select your iPhone under Devices at the left side of the screen.

Right-click on your device and choose Restore from backup

How to sync iPhone SE2020 with iTunes

Using a USB cable, connect your iPhone with the computer.

Be sure to have the latest version of iTunes installed and running before you restore

Open iTunes and select your iPhone under Devices, click the summary tab and select sync with this (device) over Wi-Fi then click apply

How to set Date and Time

Be sure you are running in the latest iOS version on the iPhone SE 2020

Tap the Settings app from the home screen, select General and choose Date & Time, this and should automatically set your date and time based on your current time zone; however, if there be an available time zone update, your iPhone will notify you.

How to set up Contacts, Mails, and Calendar Accounts on iPhone SE 2020.

The first step is to set up a mail account because this mail account automatically updates the calendar account most times.

To set up Mail, tap the Settings app from the home screen, select Account, and select your choice services. Enter your email and password; however, if you had a 2-factor authentication turned on, you will be asked for that.

Once the Account is linked, select the services you wish to enable. Email is automatically activated, and you can choose to allow calendar and contacts sync for the enabled Account.

After this, just open the mail app and wait for new emails to appear.

If the service of your choice isn't apple mail, your mails may not be displayed on the notification board when it comes in; therefore, you have to do an extra step.

From the mail section in settings, select the preferred Account, and tap 'Fetch New Data.'

Set it to how frequent you want your notifications to pop up

How to Set up Contact

To set up Contact, tap the Phone app from the home screen, tap Contacts, and tap the Add +icon.

Enter the contact details and tap add phone, and that's the end. However, If you want to add a contact from the call log, tap the Phone app from the home screen and select Recently. Select the Info icon next to the desired number, and choose either Create New Contact or add to Existing Contact and follow the preceding instructions

How to Make a call on iPhone SE 2020

Open the Phone app from the home screen, tap Keypad and enter the number you want to dial then tap the call button. If you wish to change Line, tap the Line atop the screen and select your preferred line.

How to answer a phone call on iPhone SE 2020

When you have an incoming call, you can decide to either answer it or silence it. To silence the incoming call, press the bottom volume button. This silence the call but call continues until it is ended or diverted. If the iPhonr screen lock is turned on tap the screen and drag the accept call icon to the right

If the screen lock is off and the call comes in, tap Accept.

To end a call, tap the end call icon and return to the home screen.

How to share photos, videos, and location

It is possible to share photos and videos from the photo app, in-mails, messages, or other apps you install. You can select your best photos or videos from an event and recommend people you wish to share.

To share a single photo or video on the iPhone, open the photo or video, tap on share, and then choose how you want to share it.

Share multiple photos or videos in 'images or days,' while viewing photos in the All photos or Days tab, tap Select and choose the photos you want to share. Tap the Share icon and choose a share option.

To share photos or videos in messages you receive from email, tap to download the item, and then tap the share icon, and choose a sharing option.

Alternatively, you can touch and hold the item, then choose a sharing or saving option.

From a Text Message, tap the photo or video in the conversation, and tap the share icon, choose a sharing a saving option.

Share location; open Apple maps touch the blue dot that indicates devices location and then Tap on the blue ShareShare my location button. Choose the app you want to use to send your location; however, if you are already following travel directions in apple maps, swipe it up on the bottom of the screen, tap on share ETA, then choose a contact you may want to share your ETA with during your journey. Once you reach your destination, your location will stop broadcasting too.

Important Message setting

In the messages app, you can send and receive SMS/MMS messages through your cellular service or with iMessage over Wi-Fi or cellular service to people who use the iPhone. iMessage text can include photos, videos, and other info. Also documents you send or receive using iMessage do not count against your SMS/MMS allowances in your cellular messaging plan; however, cellular data rates may apply.

To sign in iMessages, open the Settings app from the home screen and turn on iMessage.

Sign in to iMessage on your iPhone and other Apple devices using the same Apple ID. If you sign in to iMessage with the same Apple ID on all your devices, all the messages that you send and receive on your iPhone will also show on your other Apple device.

Send a message from whichever device is closest to you to start a conversation.

How to set up iCloud Drive on iPhone SE 2020

When you store files in iCloud Drive, it stays up to date across all your other devices, and you can access them anytime and anywhere. Any data you store on iCloud Drive cannot be lost even when you lose your iPhone.

How to set up iCloud Drive on iPhone SE

To set up iCloud Drive, ensure that your iPhone is updated to the latest iOS, be sure you are signed in to iCloud with the same Apple ID on all your other devices. To begin, tap on settings from your iPhone home screen, select iCloud and turn on iCloud Drive, and find your iCloud-Drive files in the Files app.

How to set up Apple ID on the iPhone SE

Apple ID is an account that allows you to access some iPhone features on the iPhone SE2. Such as; download and installation of apps and games from the App Store, purchasing Music, movies, and books from iTunes, sync Calenders, Reminders and Contact through iCloud, and use FaceTime and imessages in the Message apps. Although it is possible to use an iPhone without having an Apple ID, it is necessary to utilize its amazing features.

To create a new Apple ID, tap the Setting app from the home screen. At the top of the screen, tap Sign in to your iPhone, and select either Don't Have an Apple ID, or Forgot It. Tap create Apple ID when the window pops up, enter a birth date, and other required fields. Agree to the Terms and Conditions. Tap Merge or Don't Merge to sync iCloud data from Safari, reminders, contacts, and calendars and tap OK to confirm the Find My iPhone feature is on.

How to sign in iCloud with existing Apple ID

To sign in with the existing Apple ID on your iPhone SE 2, tap the Settings app from the home screen. Tap Sign in to your iPhone at the top of the screen, enter the email address and password associated with your Apple ID and tap Sign in and type your iPhone passcode or Touch ID if you have one set up.

How to sign out of iCloud on iPhone SE 2020

Tap the Settings app, touch your Apple ID at the top of the screen, and then scroll to the bottom and then tap Sign Out. Enter the password associated with your Apple ID and tap Turn Off. Select which file you want to keep a copy of on the iPhone SE 2 and toggle the switch on. In the upper right corner, tap Sign Out and when prompted to confirm you want to sign out of iCloud on your iPhone SE 2

How to Arrange your Apps

To move your apps around the home screen to arrange them or keep them in folders, tap and hold it on the home screen; at this, the app starts to jiggle. To move the app, tap, and drag to the new location, you want it to be. This location could be on the same page, another page, or the dock at the bottom of the screen.

To know how many pages you have, look at the small dots above the dock, as it indicates which of the page you are currently viewing. When you finish moving the apps, press the home button.

How to Organize Folders on the iPhone SE 2020

To create a folder that you can use to organize your apps on the home screen for more straightforward navigation, tap and hold or long-press any app on your home screen and tap Edit Home Screen. Then drag any app to the other like you want to place them on each other. This action automatically creates a folder. These folders are unnamed by default; therefore, to rename it, tap the place where you have the name and enter the preferred name. When you finish, press the home button.

How to Change Wallpapers

To change wallpapers on your iPhone, tap the Setting and select Wallpaper, tap Choose New Wallpaper.

You can choose from pre-set images, your photo, and so on. After you make your choice, you can reposition or just proceed. Tap set, select either Set Lock Screen, Set Home Screen or Set Both, and press the home button to finish up.

How to Change the Screen Brightness and Color Balance

To adjust the screen brightness, tap the Settings app from the home screen, select display & brightness, and drag the slider to adjust the screen brightness manually.

To adjust it automatically, tap the Settings app from the home screen and select Accessibility, then tap Display & text Size, now turn on Auto-Brightness.

How to use Voice Control on the iPhone SE

To turn on the voice control feature, tap the Setting app from the home screen, tap Accessibility, and select Voice Control, now, select Set up Voice Control. This action will prompt a voice control to start in the background. When this download finishes, a microphone icon will appear in the status bar of the iPhone SE 2. It is important to note that voice control doesn't affect how the iPhone reacts to touch.

To use the voice control feature, make sure the voice control is on the iPhone SE 2 and just say commands like 'swipe down,' 'place a call.'

How to change the language for voice control

To change the language for the voice control feature, tap the Settings app from the home screen, tap General, and then tap International. Select Voice Control and choose the language you want.

How to search for anything on the iPhone SE using the search bar

Search for anything using the search bar, swipe down from the middle of the home screen, and tap the Search area. Fill in your search key or what you want to search meanwhile as you are filling in your search key; the result shows in real-time. When you finish filling in your search key, tap Show More and select a search result by touching it.

How to access the Control Center on the iPhone SE

To open and access the control center on the iPhone SE2020, swipe up from the bottom edge of the screen or simply press the home button.

How to Add and Remove Control Center icons

To customize the control center, tap the Settings app from the home screen and select Control Center, then tap Customize Controls. To add icons tap the add button, but when removing an icon, tap the remove button and then tap Remove. To rearrange the icons, tap and hold the three gray lines next to the controls and drag to where you want.

How to activate the Do Not Disturb feature.

Whenever the Do Not Disturb feature is on, you will notice a crescent moon in the status bar, and also does not affect alarms. There are two ways to activating the do not disturb feature.

Tap the Settings app from the home screen; select Do Not Disturb to turn it on. Alternatively, press the home button to display the control center, tap it on/off, or tap and hold the crescent moon icon to adjust the do not disturb settings.

How to turn ON access restrictions on iPhone SE

Restrictions are otherwise known as parental control and to set restrictions, tap the Settings app from the home scrccn, and select Screentime then tap turn on Screentime. Now tap Content & Privacy restrictions and fill in a four-digit passcode, input the passcode again to confirm it. You can now select which of the contents to block. Tap Done when you finish.

How to use Airplay on the iPhone SE

To use Airplay, ensure your device support Airplay or meets the requirements. Then add your Apple TV or Airplay 2-compatible smart TV to the Home app and assign it to a room. Connect the iPhone SE 2020 to the same Wi-Fi as the Apple TV or any compatible TV, find the video you want to play and tap the share icon

How to Use AirPrint on the iPhone SE

Ensure your printer supports Airprint and connect both your iPhone and printer to the same Wi-Fi network and also within range.

Launch the app you want to print from and tap the share icon to find the print option, scroll down to get the print option, and tap it. Tap Select Printer and choose an AirPrint-enabled printer. Select the number of copies along with some other print options and tap print at the top right corner

How to use FaceTime

To use Facetime, you can merely as Siri, saying something like 'make a Facetime call' or open the Contact app and place a call or choose a contact from the list of Facetime calls to make a call. If you want to call several persons on the go, make a group Facetime call. If your call recipient misses your call, just tap on the screen to leave a message, tap Cancel to end the call.

Make adjustments to your Facetime feature, tap the Settings app from the home screen, select Facetime, and then turn on Facetime and change other settings based on preference.

CHAPTER TEN

Troubleshooting Common Issues on the iPhone SE

How to Force Restart the iPhone SE 2

To Force Restart the iPhone SE, press and release the volume button, do the same with the volume-down button. Next, press and hold-down the side button till the apple logo comes on and release it.

How to Fix iPhone SE not responding to touch

If your iPhone SE 2 does not respond to touch, tap, and hold the home button along with the sleep/wake button at the same time for 10-15 seconds. This action will restart the phone, and it should start responding; however, if it doesn't still work, check for physical damages or water contact.

How to fix iPhone SE not charging

If your iPhone SE 2 is not charging, ensure you have tried both wireless charging and with USB adapter/ cable. If it still isn't charging do the following

Ensure your lighting cable and adapter is not damage anywhere.

- Try a different power outlet
- Clean your iPhone charging port
- Let it charge for 30 minutes
- Force restart the phone
- Let it charge for another 30 minutes

If it still doesn't come on take the iPhone SE 2 to an Apple Retail Store

How to fix iPhone SE not finding network

If the iPhone SE 2 is not finding the network, ensure the area you are has cellular network coverage, and do this.

Turn on cellular/mobile data: open the Settings app from the home screen and tap cellular/mobile data to turn it on. While if you are abroad, open the Settings app from the home screen, select Cellular and select Cellular Data Options, then tap Data Roaming, Restart the iPhone. It should find network now, if not ensure the following; check for carrier settings, check the SIM card, reset network settings, update to the latest iOS, contact carrier.

How to fix iPhone SE frozen Screen

If your iPhone screen is frozen, try to Force Star the iPhone; however, if that doesn't work, press an release the up volume button, do the same for th down volume button, then long-press the powe button until the device restarts. Plug your device t power and allow it to charge for up to an hour.

How to recover a stolen iPhone SE

To recover a stolen iPhone, you can either use Fin My app or the web. To use the Internet, sign in t iCloud.com/find on the web and tap Find iPhon then select the iPhone SE to view its curren location. You can now the iPhone as lost; this wi remotely lock the iPhone SE with a passcode, trac the device's location, and suspend the ability t make payments. Talk to your local lav enforcement about your stolen iPhone.

How to fix iPhone SE that won't turn ON.

If your iPhone SE won't turn on, the first thing t check the iPhone's body, look out for any physic damage and confirm it didn't get in contact wit liquid. And this is because although the iPhone S is water-resistant when you expose it to water intentionally or any liquid for a prolonged period, it can be damaged. Secondly, ensure it is not a battery/charging issue, plug in the charger, and leave for about 5 minutes while ensuring all your charging gears are intact. If it still doesn't come on, unplug the charger. And lastly, try to Force Restart the phone. Because if it is a firmware crash, troubleshooting will be the best option. However, if after doing the above, your iPhone SE 2 still won't turn on, call an Apple tech, or just make an appointment with a qualified tech to get professional help.

Printed in Great Britain
by Amazon

77470480R00068

NURSING – IMAGE

50p

MODERN NURSING SERIES

General Editors

A J HARDING RAINS, MS, FRCS
Regional Dean, British Postgraduate Medical Federation,
formerly Professor of Surgery, Charing Cross Hospital Medical School
Honorary Consultant Surgeon to the Army

MISS VALERIE HUNT, SRN, SCM, OND, RNT
Formerly District Nursing Officer, Avon Health Authority (Teaching)

MISS SUSAN E NORMAN, SRN, NDN Cert, RNT
Tutor for Staff Development, The Nightingale School, St Thomas's Hospital,
London

This Series caters for the needs of a wide range of nursing, medical and ancillary professions. Some of the titles are given below, but a complete list is available from the Publisher.

Gerontology and Geriatric Nursing
SIR W FERGUSON ANDERSON, OBE, KstJ, MD, FRCP
F I CAIRD, MA, DM, FRCP
R D KENNEDY, MB, ChB, FRCP
DORIS SCHWARTZ

Rheumatology
D R SWINSON, MB, BS, MRCP
W R SWINBURN, MB, MRCP

Psychology and Psychiatry
PETER J DALLY, MB, FRCP, DPM

Textbook of Medicine
with relevant physiology and anatomy
R J HARRISON, ChB, MD

Medicine, Surgery and Nursing – Multiple Choice Questions and Answers
R J HARRISON, ChB, MD

Community Health and Social Services
J B MEREDITH DAVIES, MD, FFCM, DPH

Sociology in Medicine
R KENNETH JONES, BA, PhD, ACE
PATRICIA JONES, SRN

Venereology and Genito-Urinary Medicine
R D CATTERALL, FRCPE, FRCP

Neurology
EDWIN R BICKERSTAFF, MD, MRCP

NURSING – IMAGE OR REALITY?

Margaret C Schurr
SRN, NA Cert, Cert Ed

Janet Turner
SRN SCM DipN, DANS, RCNT

HODDER AND STOUGHTON

LONDON SYDNEY AUCKLAND TORONTO

British Library Cataloguing in Publication Data

Schurr, Margaret C.
   Nursing – image or reality?
   1. Nursing – Social aspects
   I. Title   II. Turner, Janet
   306.4   RT86.5

ISBN 0 340 28186 3

First published 1982

Copyright © 1982 M. C. Schurr and Janet Turner

All rights reserved. No part of this publication may be reproduced
or transmitted in any form or by any means, electronic, or mechanical,
including photocopy, recording, or any information storage or retrieval
system, without permission in writing from the publisher.

Photo Typeset by Macmillan India Ltd., Bangalore.

Printed in Great Britain for
Hodder and Stoughton Educational,
a division of Hodder and Stoughton Ltd,
Mill Road, Dunton Green, Sevenoaks, Kent
by Richard Clay (The Chaucer Press) Ltd. Bungay, Suffolk.

Editors' Foreword

The scope of this series has increased since it was first established, and it now serves a wide range of medical, nursing and ancillary professions, in line with the present trend towards the belief that all who care for patients in a clinical context have an increasing amount in common.

The texts are carefully prepared and organised so that they may be readily kept up to date as the rapid developments of medical science demand. The series already includes many popular books on various aspects of medical and nursing care, and reflects the increased emphasis on community care.

The increasing specialisation in the medical profession is fully appreciated and the books are often written by physicians or surgeons in conjunction with specialist nurses. For this reason, they will not only cover the syllabus of training of the General Nursing Council, but will be designed to meet the needs of those undertaking training controlled by the Joint Board of Clinical Studies.

About the authors

Margaret Schurr has had wide experience of teaching management to nurses, especially those close to the patient. She has held senior nursing posts in London and Sheffield, and worked for two years in the Nursing Division of the Department of Health. *Janet Turner*, formerly Nursing Officer at The Royal Hallamshire Hospital, Sheffield, is studying for her MSc at the Department of Nursing Studies, University of Manchester.

Acknowledgements

In recording our appreciation of all those who have assisted us in the writing of this book, we should first like to thank our editors, and in particular Miss Valerie Hunt for her encouragement and helpful criticism.

For the typing of the manuscripts we owe a great debt to Miss Joan Witts and Miss Susan Bradney for their skilled and careful work. We are also indebted to the librarians of the School of Nursing, Exeter District Health Authority, and the reference department of the Torquay library, for their ready help and interest.

We are grateful to all the individuals and organisations who so readily agreed to the use of references and quotations, and would especially mention Professor A G Johnson, and Mr B P Bliss for permission to quote from their book *Aims and Motives in Clinical Medicine*, and also Mrs Helen Orton who allowed us to refer to her research into the ward learning climate. We acknowledge the opportunity given to us by the staff of the School of Nursing, Le Bons Secours Hospital, Geneva, to study their philosophy in relation to the educational programme for student nurses.

Finally, our thanks must be to all those who have helped us to shape our philosophy during our nursing experience, and have enabled us to share this with others.

Margaret C Schurr
Janet Turner

*Dedicated to Valerie Hunt with
our affection and gratitude*

Preface

What should nurses achieve, what is their goal? It is important to ask these questions in order that the role of the nurse can be defined and understood. In our attempts to explore these questions we have brought a common philosophy but very different experience. Our book is intended to help other members of the profession in their search for the true meaning of nursing, and to stimulate thoughts about the future role of the nurse in relation to the needs of society.

Inevitably, in the course of our questioning, attitudes toward nursing have been challenged, the preparation of nurses examined, and the management of the nursing service scrutinised. The book should therefore be of interest not only to nurses, but to those of other professions who work alongside them, and to students preparing for medicine and nursing.

Changes in society and in the health service have affected the role of nurses, and make it essential that it should be re-examined. During the last ten years nurses have become more aware of their own professional identity and of the impact of other professionals. Social and economic changes have meant that values may be challenged. Nurses are now required to substantiate the reasons for adhering to criteria which hitherto have been accepted without question as being essential for maintaining standards of nursing care. Advances in technology have made increasing demands on nurses, and have required them to extend their responsibilities and their influence.

The role of the nurse can be enlarged or restricted according to the philosophy held by the leaders, and also the shape of the organisational structure. However, perhaps too much emphasis has been placed on the pattern of management. The structure is only a framework, what really matters is the contribution made by the people within it towards a common goal. By concentrating on the objectives, it should be possible to define how the roles and relationships fit together. The nurse has a unique contribution within a multidisciplinary team, and this must be recognised if the individual needs of patients are to be satisfied.

In Part I of the book it is emphasised that the true content of nursing should bear a direct relation to these individual needs. The subject is broadened in Part I to include the activity of the nurse within society as a whole, and which goes beyond the actual giving of care. The final section presents an answer to the question who is this Nurse? and, in defining the role, the emphasis is on the attributes and attitudes which are required. Although it may be difficult to measure these, some practical suggestions are included to show how this can be done, and how the standards of performance can be controlled.

We do not presume to have all the answers to the many questions which face the profession. However, we believe that the principles and the philosophy which have been identified are universal and fundamental. They can be applied in whatever circumstances nurses make their contribution.

By interpreting the content of nursing as suggested in this book, it is possible to work toward a better quality of communication between the nurse, the patient, his family, and all members of the caring team. This is the only foundation for a relationship of mutual trust and understanding, which is the essence of professionalism.

Authors' Note

Within the text reference to 'patients' includes anybody who requires the services of a nurse, and does not only reflect hospital care. For clarity only, 'patient' rather than 'patient or client' has been used throughout.

Contents

PART I

The Role of the Nurse

A Philosophy of Nursing

Nursing is concerned with caring for people throughout the span of life. It is founded on the belief that every person merits equal care and attention; has individual rights, preferences, needs, beliefs, emotions and problems unique to him or to her.

Considering each person's individuality and the physical, psychological and spiritual aspects of daily life, the nurse assesses how a patient's need for care may be met by planned nursing intervention; ensures this care is provided and evaluates the results.

The nurse enables a patient to reach his potential health, well-being and comfort, using a cognitive and imaginative approach to solving problems.

By assessment and recognition of specialist skills required in meeting the total needs of each patient, the nurse communicates with, and co-ordinates the membership of a fluctuating team, which may include the patient and his 'family'.

Nurses have a responsibility for the promotion and maintenance of good health and the prevention of ill health by education and example.

I

What is Nursing?

Concepts of care

'Surely all that is needed of a nurse is someone who cares?'
This question was asked by a member of the public, but it is not
unknown for nurses themselves to express the same sentiment.
What is the role of the nurse? What is meant by nursing? Perhaps the
even harder question is, what is meant by care?

In an attempt to answer these questions, it is necessary to look at
nursing as an aspect of society. Society, of which nurses are
members, will change, as will the values and expectations of those
whom nurses serve. However, there are fundamentals which are
constant, and which are essential for the satisfaction of human needs.
As more diseases are eradicated, prevented or controlled, the
concept of health is changing. It is no longer seen to be merely the
absence of illness, but a state of complete well-being. This alters the
objectives of those giving health care, and also the expectations of
the recipients. Now, the main aim is not simply to nurse for
survival, but to promote and maintain the highest possible quality of
life . . . the state of health until death.

This concept of care emphasises the existence of two components,
those related to medical diagnosis, and those related to personal
needs, irrespective of the diagnosis. To ensure that both these aspects
are met, the role of the nurse is that of co-ordinator. However,
although many duties may be delegated to them by other
professionals, *it is nurses who make the decisions which are centred on the
achievement of the nursing objectives.* For example, the doctor who has
made a diagnosis will expect a certain pattern of nursing care
associated with the management of the medical treatment prescribed, and the physiotherapist will require the patient to have had
adequate analgesia to enable effective therapy to be given. Both
these requirements will be fulfilled by the nurse, but differentiation
is needed between this medically-directed care and the nursing care
which is prescribed by nurses themselves. If emphasis is placed on
medically-orientated care only, the content of nursing will be seen
in terms of a series of tasks associated with certain aspects of disease,
rather than a personal service to satisfy individual human needs.

Florence Nightingale wrote in her *Notes on Nursing*:[1]

4

Nursing . . . has been limited to signify little more than the administration of medicines or the application of poultices.

Replace the word poultice with dressing, and very little may have changed since 1859.

It is possible, in these circumstances, to see the content of nursing care as being associated merely with technical procedures and tasks aimed at meeting the hygienic and physical needs of patients; doing for them or assisting them with those everyday activities which cannot be done independently. Many of these tasks taken in isolation are very simple and routine, even monotonous, and may not be considered to require any specialist nursing skills. However, in assisting patients with their most basic physical needs, nurses are often placed in a privileged position. This allows the scope of their care to be widened, as they seek new ways of meeting the emotional, psychological, social and spiritual needs of those for whom they care.

This broader concept of nursing care is therefore concerned with people as individuals, not just 'patients'. This is well illustrated by the comments of a man admitted to three different hospitals during the course of his illness. In contrasting his reception at each hospital and the care he received, he observed,

I see a difference between a patient and a person, although inevitably they are physically the same. A person has an identity particular to himself, whilst a patient has, in many cases, particulars peculiar to a specific illness.[2]

This may seem obvious, but it is doubtful if present nursing practice always *allows* for the nursing of patients as people, so that provision can be made to meet all that being human entails and demands.

The true concept of nursing

It is this assessment and the interpretation of individual need which may be aided, alleviated and even prevented by the nurse, and which requires sophisticated skills. These, together with the planning and evaluation of care form the crux of modern nursing. They make the role of the nurse unique, complex and exciting. Nursing thus embraces the process of assisting, enabling and supporting patients, together with those people important to them, in order that they can make an adjustment to a period of ill health, come to terms with the effects of their illness, or die with dignity.

This concept of the role of the nurse reaches out to all types of health care, and will not always be fulfilled by clinical involvement. By giving advice, teaching and assisting not only patients, but others who care for them, nurses extend their contribution beyond the narrow confines of sickness to the promotion and the sustaining of health.

The management of patient care

The reluctance among nurses to consider alternative concepts of care, has resulted in a delay in taking positive steps to take a fresh look at the methods by which it is given, and to assess whether or not these are effective. Some attempts towards change are being made, but there are not enough precise definitions of the methods by which patient care is organised. Such terms as 'team nursing', 'patient allocation,' and more recently 'the nursing process', are interchanged as if they have the same meaning. The most common approach, has been to allocate a series of tasks for nurses to perform. This pattern allows little opportunity for building relationships, and patients are therefore unable to participate readily in decisions about their nursing care. In her study entitled *The Unpopular Patient* F. Stockwell[3] observed that nurse—patient contact in the wards was almost without exception task-orientated, implying that patients who do not need to receive actual physical care will have no contact with nurses. One of the factors which distinguished the popular patients in this study, was their ability to attract the attention of nurses in order to initiate conversation. Evaluation of standards is extremely difficult in these circumstances, since if the patient is unable to make suggestions which *he* feels are necessary for his well-being, it is unlikely that his total needs will be satisfied. Lip service is paid to 'total care' implying that personal needs *are* met, but unfortunately the facts do not always support this. All too often 'good nursing' is seen as that which satisfies the nurse, embracing the completion of a work load according to the established routine. This satisfaction is also registered if the patient behaves according to the accepted pattern, and conforms to the expectations of the nurse.

Lack of staff, finance, or time, may be given as reasons for retaining the present system, when they are often merely excuses. The real problem lies in an inability to recognise that the expectations of those receiving care are not always compatible with that which is provided.

The hierarchy of tasks

There has always been a tendency to allot status symbols to tasks within nursing and to give prestige to certain procedures, regardless of their importance to the patient. This has sometimes influenced the goals which nurses pursue. Many of the issues which deflect energy and thought from a positive contribution to the quality of nursing, could be overcome by considering those factors which are most important to the patient. These may include aspects which nurses hitherto have considered to be of low priority, and indeed which they have delegated to auxiliary and untrained helpers. Until nurses are convinced that it is as necessary to study which type of bedding gives the maximum comfort, as it is to understand the complexity of a parenteral infusion, nursing will lack those essentials which truly satisfy those receiving care.

The essential teamwork

When the emphasis changes from curing to caring, no one professional group has total responsibility for the management of care, or can provide all the solutions to the wide range of problems which can occur. The appropriate practitioners combine to form a multidisciplinary team to meet each particular situation, and individual members will be involved because of their specific skills and knowledge. On occasions there will inevitably be an overlap of duties and responsibilities. In order that resources are used to the best advantage it is necessary that the initiative is taken by the person best suited and available when help is required. Such flexibility need not produce confusion if there is goodwill, and if the members of the team have confidence in one another.

The team can also extend its usefulness by the sharing of expertise. Nurses have much to give of their knowledge and experience, and they, in turn, can learn from their colleagues in other disciplines. It is a two-way process based on mutual respect for what each individual has to offer. It is this sharing which welds the team together into an integrated whole and enhances its effectiveness. In no way does it detract from the acknowledged ability of the experts in their particular field.

It is hoped that in the process of reading this book, nurses will take a fresh look at their own concepts of nursing care, and examine these alongside those which are contained in the following chapters. If some of the ideas appear new, and unrealistic, it is wise before discarding them to reconsider some of the prevailing attitudes about nursing, and to make sure that these are not outdated. Unless this is done, there is a danger that the kind of nurse who will be needed by the public in the future may remain only an image, and never become a reality.

References

1   Nightingale, F. 1859. *Notes on Nursing: What it is and What it is not.* Editions include Blackie, Glasgow, 1974; Dover, London, 1970 (paperback); Duckworth, London, 1970 (facsimile).
2   Report of the Rcn working committee on standards of nursing care. 1981. *Nursing Times,* 9 April.
3   Stockwell, F. 1973. *The Unpopular Patient.* London: Rcn.

2

The Fundamentals of Nursing

A personal philosophy

Nurses have been given the responsibility of caring for other people. The extent to which they accept this responsibility depends upon their personal philosophy and beliefs about the nature of man and the nature of nursing. This in turn will be affected by the perception nurses have of their role and the degree of their awareness of themselves as individuals.

Nurses are usually seen as practical and busy people. Often patients and their relatives, and even nurses, are heard to say, 'They seem so busy', 'They have not the time'. The nurse's image is that of 'doer' rather than 'thinker' and it is not surprising therefore that there is a reluctance to discuss the 'why' rather than the 'how' of nursing.

A philosophy is a statement of beliefs and values which motivate actions in a certain way. It is abstract and immeasurable, but is the essential basis for setting goals and objectives. However, the objectives themselves are statements of intention and these are measurable. The philosophy of care will be seen in practice in the objectives which nurses set for themselves, and for their patients.

If a nurse's personal philosophy is based upon respect for the inherent individuality of every patient, this will be reflected in the care which is planned. Patients will not be seen within the isolation of a diagnosis, but within their normal environment and culture. The care planned will take into account the unique preferences, beliefs, emotional needs and problems of each individual. It will also take into consideration the patient's genetic, physical and psychological make-up. This belief in the uniqueness of each man and woman has implications for the daily decisions which the nurse has to make. It may be easy to state a philosophy that all men are individuals, and therefore merit equal care and attention. It is much more difficult to put this into practice because there are conflicts. It is easier to apply the belief in man's worth to the innocent victim of a road accident than to the drunken driver of the car, when both are brought into the Accident and Emergency Department.

The nurse's reaction to the demands for care

If there is a firm conviction that the extent of caring cannot be restricted to meeting only the physical needs of patients, much more than manual dexterity and the correct completion of nursing procedures is required. To understand the wider implications nurses need not only sensitivity to people's feelings, but imagination in responding to them. To be interested in, and have concern and even affection for others, involves personal feelings and emotions on the part of the nurse. This is something which in the past has often been suppressed because too close an involvement was thought to be harmful, and too demanding for the nurse. It is true that involvement with the patient may be stressful, and therefore the nurse's environment must be supportive, and include a means of obtaining readily the necessary counselling.

To empathise with a patient we need to be able to see the person within, and imagine his feelings by putting ourselves in his place. There is only one person who really knows what is happening to the patient, and that is the patient himself. It has been known for patients to be left to cry in pain because the staff believed that nothing could go wrong with the minor operation which had been performed, and that the patients were only making a fuss. The pain is what the patient feels, not what the nurse or doctor think he should feel. The story is told of the nurse who saved someone's life, not by the skilful use of the resuscitation equipment, but by showing, quite spontaneously, that she cared about him. A man who had been involved in a road accident was taken into the Accident and Emergency Department. His normal smart appearance was hidden beneath dirt and torn clothing; he was in a great deal of pain, and at such a low ebb that he only wanted to die. A young nurse came to him. She took one look at him, gave him a kiss on his dirty forehead, and murmured quietly 'Poor old thing' — he then began to fight for his life.

Meeting the patient half-way

Nursing involves the development of relationships between people placed in certain roles. The role of the nurse is taken by choice, and that of the patient usually because of circumstances beyond his control — and almost certainly without choice. The way in which patients and nurses perceive their role will influence the interaction between them and nursing care will not become completely effective until a common understanding is reached. It cannot be assumed that because patients are willing to accept health care, they automatically agree to comply with that which is planned. Decisions should be shared so that there is active co-operation in developing and implementing nursing care.

Patients may be eager to be involved in this way and want to know about both nursing and medical matters. They may question normal practices and believe this is their right. Alternatively, they may see their role as being a very passive one and be happy to allow others to decide what is to be done, especially if they feel too ill to make the effort. Without mutual understanding there will be occasions when it may appear that a patient is being unco-operative and unresponsive, or that the nurse is unhelpful. However, if the underlying philosophy of care is discussed with patient and family, it is possible to elicit their expectations and to share objectives.

It may be difficult for the nurse to envisage this shared decision-making, since in the past the pattern has been for a much more autocratic approach – the patient conforming to whatever is suggested. In helping the patient and the relatives to come to the most appropriate decision, there is the danger that a judgement is made only in the light of the nurse's own attitude to the situation and past experience. Circumstances which seem intolerable to some, may be quite acceptable to others. In her anxiety to consider the quality of life for an unmarried daughter who was caring for her elderly mother, a nurse made strenuous efforts to persuade the family to seek residential accommodation for the patient instead of a return to her home. It was overlooked that the daughter gained fulfilment and satisfaction from undertaking this responsibility, even though it limited her opportunities to do other things; and that her mother benefitted from the love and security she received within her own home.

Developing the nurse – patient relationship

If nurses are to have an impact upon the lives of those for whom they care, the interaction between them must have meaning and purpose, and must be built upon mutual trust. For this to happen, nurses require self-confidence, and well-developed social skills. They must believe that sitting, talking and listening form an essential part of nursing time, to be planned and valued by the participants. Only by establishing effective communication will this type of relationship be created. A patient once told a ward sister that when she had come to his bedside with a chair, he knew that she was going to spend time just with him and did not intend to be interrupted. This was because she made it obvious that she was prepared to sit down and to give her whole attention. In doing so, the sister showed her caring attitude, and provided an opportunity for the patient to unburden himself, to ask questions, and seek the reassurance he required.

The need for a plan of care

In the same way that sitting and listening to a patient is an essential part of actual nursing care, so too is the development of the care plan. This will be a permanent but not static record, for it must always be relevant and dynamic. Because plans are prepared for individuals, no two will be alike. Alongside the care plan the patient's response must be stated in order that the effect of previous care can be taken into consideration. Anything which has been found to be ineffective or harmful in the past can then be excluded. No plan can be made without assessment of the nursing needs, nor is it complete without evaluation. Neither of these skills is easy, but their acquisition poses the greatest challenge to nurses at the present time.

Involving the family

A patient may be admitted to hospital having been previously expertly cared for at home by a member of his family. Both are often very afraid that nursing staff will 'take over' and that the previous care will be disregarded. It is appropriate that the person who has been caring for a patient who has been bedfast or confined to a wheelchair for many years, should plan the care with the patient and new nurse. Together, they can adapt tried and trusted methods within the new environment, to meet the needs of the moment.

It may be an important part of the nurse's care of a patient's family that they are encouraged to become involved if they, and the patient, wish. In the community it is assumed that a number of people may be involved in the care of one patient — family, friends and neighbours as well as the community nurse or health visitor, each person having specific responsibilities. Yet in hospital, relatives are often excluded, especially when a patient is very ill or dying. This may often be because of a lack of thought or even misguided good intentions on the part of the nurse. It is unusual for relatives to be asked if they would like to help make a patient more comfortable, or to be actively involved in the nursing care. Some situations appear more suitable than others to allow the participation of relatives. For instance, the offer of help to feed a patient appears to be more readily acceptable than helping with a patient's toilet or in changing his position. So often relatives who have sat by a patient's bedside for many long hours are asked to wait outside the room each time any nursing procedure is performed.

There are also occasions when relatives may be reluctant to express their wish to help; they may be afraid that they will be considered to be interfering or that they will cause harm because of their inexperience. This is especially pertinent in hospital, where the presence of an infusion or dressing may be a deterrent in itself. Careful explanation, with demonstration, of how to assist with care may be required.

Linking the theory and practice of nursing

In the past, the theory of nursing has been seen to be based first and foremost upon the medical model, concentrating on the signs, symptoms, diagnoses and treatment of medical conditions. The education of the nurse, or the lack of it, together with the historical and social considerations of the position of women, has made the role of the nurse appear subservient to that of the doctor. Any development or extension of the traditional role has been seen in the adoption of tasks previously considered as being the prerogative of the doctor.

Nurses' beliefs in their unique contribution to the care of a patient, in which nursing and medical skills complement each other, must be seen in their practice. However, the art needs to be supported by background knowledge to provide a sound basis for decision-making. This means that nurses need theoretical knowledge of all the sciences allied to nursing, the behavioural as well as the physical. Only in this way will they be able to validate the observations and assessments made when deciding a certain plan of care and in evaluating its success. However, these subjects must be seen as being complementary to the theory of nursing, and not the theory of nursing itself. The principles of nursing practice which are taught should be relevant, and applicable to any nursing situation, be it in a modern District General Hospital or in a tiny terraced house with no bathroom.

Towards a body of knowledge

In striving for a theory of nursing and in the actual examination of nursing practice, areas which require research can be identified. The mystery and aura surrounding nursing research is slowly fading, but sadly, much of present research findings remains little used in clinical practice. This may be a reflection of nurse training and past attitudes. Nurses have not always been encouraged to question current practices or to become 'research-minded', to seek out research projects and apply relevant findings to their particular sphere of work or patients' problems.

It is the simple unsophisticated experimentation which produces the answers to practical nursing problems. However, if the results of such practices are not shared the body of nursing knowledge remains restricted. It is sometimes through using a common article found in the home or the local shop that a problem is solved. It may not be listed among official nursing equipment or even be recognised as a nursing aid, but it is effective and brings help and comfort to the patient. A centre is required in each district where information of this kind can be obtained, so that with a pooling of ideas, the quality of nursing care can be enhanced.

The value of collecting together practical knowledge can also be recognised in the following example. H. Howarth when investigating the giving of mouth care, found that the methods used at present are ineffective.[1] Her research does not provide any direct answers, but raises issues for further investigation. This questions the relevance of procedure manuals. How many of the set methods are in fact practical in all situations? Instead of Procedure Committees, a group of nurses in an area could study one aspect of patient care and the various ways in which specific needs are met. It would not be difficult for a file to be made of all the different problems encountered, and how these are overcome. This would identify which methods prove effective, and which do not. The information could then be collated, and the procedure manual would become a lively reference of a variety of approaches to nursing care, rather than a set of rituals. If, in the process, other problems are identified and new ways of meeting them are found, these could easily be added. This would provide a record of *what is actually being done* and is effective, so that knowledge of the *art* of nursing can be built up. As a personal and professional obligation, nurses must adopt this analytical and critical approach, so that care remains effective, and meets the present as well as the future needs of those who receive their care.

Reference

1   Howarth, H. 1977. Mouth care procedures for the very ill. *Nursing Times*, 10 March.

3

The Practice of Nursing

Rediscovering the patient

They have done good to my body, but great harm to my spirit.

These words were said by a patient on leaving hospital. They provide a poignant reminder that the physical and emotional needs of a patient are inseparable, and of equal importance. The nurse's goal should be to provide the care which will meet effectively *all* nursing needs. This aim can only be fulfilled if the individual requirements of each patient have been identified and the care planned around them.

This concept of total nursing care is illustrated in Fig. 3.1. For convenience it has been divided into direct and indirect care, but the two are inseparable.

It is imperative to identify the specific problems of each patient at the outset, in order to know what the nursing objectives should be. Continuous revision of the problems will be required throughout

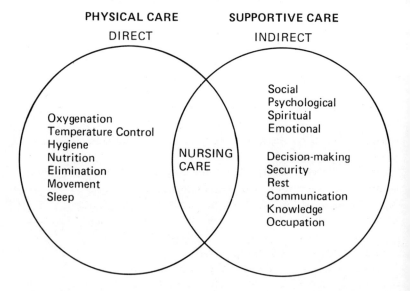

PHYSICAL CARE   **SUPPORTIVE CARE**

DIRECT   INDIRECT

Oxygenation
Temperature Control
Hygiene
Nutrition
Elimination
Movement
Sleep

NURSING CARE

Social
Psychological
Spiritual
Emotional

Decision-making
Security
Rest
Communication
Knowledge
Occupation

Fig 3.1   Individual needs to be met by nursing care

the period that the patient requires nursing assistance so that these objectives can be modified or changed as necessary. So often in the past, plans have been made founded upon presumptions, and probably designed according to a traditional routine based upon a medical diagnosis, or perhaps the particular whims of the doctor or the nurse.

The objectives must be stated clearly and be measurable. Statements that are vague are liable to misinterpretation, and can only result in nursing care which is also ill-defined. For example, the nursing objective for a patient who has suffered from a varicose ulcer may be to lose some body weight, in order to prevent further problems regarding her varicose veins. However, to merely state 'loss of weight' as the objective would be useless if the patient has not accepted or understood the need to do so. The primary and short-term goal will therefore be to understand why the patient has a weight problem, and her attitude to it. It could be that the patient is eating inappropriate food because of financial difficulties, in which case some thought must be given to advocating a diet which will reduce weight but not send up the housekeeping bill. Having achieved this first objective, the next step will be to help the patient to understand the type of diet which will serve her best. It is only at this stage, after precise initial goals have been determined, that progress can be made toward the main objective. It is also more likely that it will be achieved, since the patient's interest and co-operation will be forthcoming.

Nursing objectives will not be attained unless attention is given to the method by which they are communicated. Not only must they be clearly stated, they must also be passed on to the appropriate member of staff, who in the instance just described, would be the dietitian. In a recent article in a nursing journal[1] a student nurse described her efforts to build up effective communication with a deaf and visually handicapped patient before he underwent a surgical operation. She learnt the manual sign language in order to achieve her objective. Unfortunately, when he returned from the operating theatre, the patient's intravenous infusion was being administered into his 'talking hand' and this meant that the manual sign language had to be done on the other hand, causing much confusion. This can be considered as just lack of thought, but the problem could have been averted if the nursing objectives had been shared with the operating theatre staff.

The skilful use of the nursing process, namely, the assessing, planning, implementing and evaluating of the care required by each patient, allows an opportunity for nurses to put into practice a belief in the inherent individuality of every patient. Although it has yet to be proved that this *is* the best method, it does provide a sensible approach, and highlights the areas which at present are weak in nursing practice. Even without complete empirical evidence, there is a sufficient number of nurses who feel it could be the framework for better care. It must be stressed, however, that the adoption of this approach as a solution to present problems cannot be contemplated without due consideration of the implications. Whilst providing some answers, the nursing process also' raises perplexing questions, and many challenges, which have relevance for all trained nurses. This is not only in the field of education, since there has to be a re-thinking of the planning of the nursing service itself if the implementation is to be successful.

Meeting the nurse's needs

Nurses have not been trained to be skilled interviewers. In general they lack the ability to ask appropriate questions and to encourage patients to talk about themselves in such a way that their relationship can be truly therapeutic. This cannot be considered to be an inherent skill, but like any other aspect of nursing, it is one which needs to be developed and supported during the initial period of nursing education, and then continuously throughout the nurse's career.

At present, it is not uncommon for student nurses to be expected to produce a comprehensive assessment of the patient's problems unsupervised. This may be because many trained nurses are unaware of the difficulties, and are unwilling to demonstrate their own lack of knowledge about the principles of the nursing process. To actually write down a nursing history is a complicated task requiring much skill in both written and verbal communication. This situation raises several questions. Who is the appropriate person to assess a patient's need and plan the care? How can these skills be taught which essentially form the basis of the art of nursing? Possibly the answers can be found in the realisation that nurses must act as 'models'. Sisters or charge nurses, staff nurses, clinical teachers and nurse tutors are required who will be willing to demonstrate how to obtain this information within a particular nursing situation. This should be done as a *planned* lesson. For example, when the nursing students from the introductory course are taken to the wards to observe the giving of a blanket bath, instead of concentrating on the routine of the task as a set procedure, students could primarily be asked to note and comment upon the interaction between the nurse and the patient — what is said and how it is said, with the emphasis on listening to what the patient is trying to convey. For this to happen there must be a sufficient number of trained and confident nurses willing to expose themselves in this way, and who will be prepared to discuss the dialogue which has taken place between them and the patient.

The somewhat autocratic image of the nurse of the past may have served as a protection against the inevitable emotional strain of a caring relationship, but if a closer involvement with the patient is to be encouraged, and to be seen as a priority, it is necessary to be sure of the extent and the limits of that relationship.

Laying more emphasis on contact with patients, rather than on the completion of routine tasks, has particular implications for the sisters and charge nurses whether working in hospitals or within the community. It will be more important than ever before to remember what it is like to be a nurse who is in the early stages of training. With the present method of ward organisation, security lies in the completion of certain duties which are well-defined and known, and which often do not change as the nurse moves from ward to ward. This can have disadvantages in that it may produce boredom, and it is not unknown for nurses to leave because they have lacked the opportunity to be personally involved in the patient's plan of care. However, to adopt the principles of the nursing process, this prop of an established pattern of work is removed, and the nurse has to learn to make decisions, for which ultimately, he or she will be accountable as a qualified person. The nurse-in-charge therefore requires both compassion and understanding, particularly during the initial stages of implementing this new type of nursing. One of the best ways of gaining sensitivity to the changes which are taking place, is to become conversant with what is required of those to whom nursing care is delegated. This means acquiring expertise in the skills of interviewing and assessment, and understanding the complex task of writing down the nursing objectives. To do this requires effort and commitment, and a new understanding of the role of the leader of the nursing team. No longer will it be necessary for all decisions about the individual care of patients to be controlled directly by the nurse-in-charge, although he or she will always remain the co-ordinator of the efforts of the team members, ensuring that each patient receives what is needed.

Assessment − overcoming the difficulties

Accurate assessment of nursing care requires a much broader concept of the content of nursing than has previously been envisaged. This can be seen by referring to Fig. 3.1. Nurses have been trained to observe, but often this is related to medical and physical signs rather than aspects of behaviour. They may only therefore see that for which they have been trained to look, and expect to see. On the other hand, it may be that they also take into consideration only what they want to see, avoiding those signs which involve a closer relationship with the patient. There may be times when it even appears that nurses forget why they are present. Whilst adhering to the 'routine' and the protection it provides, the gap between nurse and patient widens and becomes hard to bridge. Talking to patients may seem a simple exercise, but lack of encouragement to do this has often made nurses hesitant to take the initiative. Meanwhile, there is continued criticism of nurses and other members of the Health Service Organisation for their failure to communicate, and the apparent lack of understanding which they show, particularly when contact is first made with the hospital or department.

The efforts which are now being made to impress on nurses the importance of the simple but essential courtesies which stem from unity of thought and feeling, must be strenuously pursued if these problems are to be overcome. The time spent apparently only chatting to the patient may be the opportunity to gain valuable information from which to build up a picture of the newly admitted patient, and to gain insight into his usual way of life. Nurses have to gain the patient's confidence as they also convey a picture of themselves. This is the foundation of a professional relationship. However, if the level of conversation remains that of social 'chit-chat' without direction or purpose, this relationship will not remain at the correct level.

The plan of nursing care

Having gained an appreciation of the patient's problems, his reaction to his illness, and his social and cultural background, the nurse will be ready to consider the plan of nursing care. In gathering this knowledge there now has to be a sorting of the information that is relevant. It is not always easy to know when adequate detail has been assembled, and it is often just one further question and answer which would produce a more accurate understanding of the situation. This is shown in the following description of the preparation of an elderly patient for discharge from hospital to her own flat. The ward sister knew that there was not any hot water in the old block of flats where the patient lived alone, but was assured that she could boil her water on the gas stove. Twelve months later, the same patient was admitted, and when she was ready to go home again, the ward sister concluded that the same circumstances regarding the hot water supply would prevail. However, she was horrified when the patient expressed a worry about who would bring the water to the flat as she could no longer manage to do this. The sister knew there was no hot water supply, but she had never imagined that there was *no* water at all in the flat.

In providing the nursing plan, nurses should be looking ahead and anticipating the patient's requirements on going home or back to work. This is something which in the past has often been neglected. There is a skill in knowing at what point nursing assistance should be withdrawn, and the patient begin to take care of himself. Safety factors have to be considered, since the patient may fall if allowed to walk unaided. He may also overtax his new-found strength by over-exerting himself. Guidance is necessary in order that the patient may recognise when he has done sufficient for himself, and needs help. How often do nurses deter patients from making their own decisions because they are actually protecting their own interests rather than those of the patient? Some of the problem may be because once a patient no longer requires intensive nursing care, he is sometimes regarded as no longer requiring *any* nursing care and he is actually neglected beneath the guise of 'self-care'. The fact that the patient is up and about may be interpreted as being well again, and this term written in the nursing orders can mean that the patient is abandoned to look after himself. Probably what is really intended is that the patient is no longer confined to bed and can undertake some of those aspects of his care which nurses have previously done for him; but he still needs help on occasion. Unfortunately, unless this is clarified, there will be some patients who will struggle to make themselves independent, and feel guilty if they ask for assistance. It must be remembered, however, that as health improves, the psychological and emotional needs can become paramount, and may affect the patient's ability to make decisions unaided. For many people recovering from a period of ill-health, a simple decision, such as whether they will have tea or coffee to drink, may take time. This is the moment when encouragement is required to show the patient that he can do this on his own, and with tact and persuasion the range of decisions can be gradually extended.

Who is the appropriate nurse?

An important decision which has to be made by the nurse ultimately responsible for the management of care, is the assessment of the most suitable person, or persons, to provide that care for a particular patient. It may not always be the most experienced nurse who develops the most effective relationship with all the patients.

If the aim is to provide nursing for people as individuals, then the responsibility for assessing, planning and evaluating the care should lie, wherever possible, with one nurse who can be recognised by the patient and his family. It is within the concept of 'my patient — my nurse', that the wider horizons of nursing in the future are to be found. The trained nurse practitioner will be seen to be giving professional care and to be held accountable for every aspect of the nursing process. It is important to emphasise that each part of the process is of equal significance, and that if one part is omitted or devalued, the quality of nursing will suffer.

Evaluation

This is an essential part of nursing which is closely related to the objectives which have been identified. By stating what the outcome should be there is a means of evaluating the 'success' of the nursing plan. It cannot be emphasised too strongly that no evaluation of worth can be made without accurate and meaningful nursing records. Nurses often appear reluctant to commit their observations and thoughts to paper, especially if it has not been possible to carry out fully a particular plan of action. This may be for a number of reasons, and is not always the fault of poor assessment or judgement.

Florence Nightingale reminds us of [2]

> . . . the necessity of recording in words from time to time, for the information of the nurse, who will not otherwise see, that he [*the patient*] cannot do this or that, which he could do a month or a year ago. What is a nurse there for if she cannot observe these things for herself? Yet I have known . . . more accidents . . . arising from this want of observation among nurses than from almost anything else.

Evaluation also has a close link with the control of nursing standards. This subject is considered in depth in the next chapter. There is an inevitable relationship between the quality of nursing care and the expected outcomes. However, difficulty is sometimes experienced in knowing what is actually being evaluated. There is a tendency to concentrate on the nursing action rather than the quality of the assessment and the success of the nursing plan.

The following illustration and the pattern of management shown in Table 3.1 may help to demonstrate this fact:

The patient, aged seventy-five years, is suffering from a fracture of the femur, which has been treated surgically. She is moved to another ward, and the nurse who is to look after her obtains the information recorded in the first column whilst putting her to bed. There are several problems, but these two are of immediate concern to the patient, and the nurse attempts to solve them.

A valuable method of evaluating care is by regular conferences with nursing colleagues and other members of the professional staff. Sometimes the patient and his family will be included. A few moments spent considering the care of a particular patient may reveal omissions and faults in nursing practice which can be avoided on other occasions. It also can produce examples of how to remedy problems which have previously been of concern, and the solutions can be applied to the benefit of other patients. However, nurses have to be prepared to make their view known and speak out when challenged about the decisions which they have made. Criticism, as long as it is constructive, can be of great value, and help all concerned to learn more about their performance. To some, this may appear as a very threatening experience, and the leader of the group needs to be skilled in giving support and encouragement to those participating.

The degree to which reliance can be placed upon the patient's satisfaction with his care, and that of the family, has to be carefully assessed, since most patients are anxious to please. The value of the comments which are made will greatly depend on the skill with which the nurse questions the patient, so that there is a useful and honest response.

Table 3.1 The relationship between nursing goals, evaluation of their attainment and control of standards

Information Obtained from Patient	Short-term Goal	Action Required	Control of Standards	Evaluation (after one week)
Cannot sleep at night ward is too noisy and too light	Enable the patient to become rested and obtain a refreshing sleep according to her normal pattern	Ask the patient how she arranged bedtime at home. Investigate ward noise/light. Obtain information from night nurse to ascertain reasons for sleeplessness, e.g., position in bed — pain? Is night sedation being given? Is this necessary or causing problems?	Is night sedation given routinely or have night nurses been given teaching on methods of inducing sleep, and an understanding of sleep patterns in the elderly? Are mattresses and pillows in good condition? Is there an understood policy regarding reduction of noise at night? Do night nurses consider elderly people 'don't mind the light' — are attitudes of caring directed rightly?	The patient is now sleeping six hours a night, waking for a short time, and sleeping again for approximately two hours — her usual pattern. She looks rested and says she feels refreshed when she wakes. No night sedation now required.
Gets indigestion after the evening meal.	Enable the patient to enjoy her food and obtain satisfying and suitable nourishment without discomfort	Find out what the patient normally has to eat, and the pattern of her meal-times. What kind of food 'disagrees' with her? Ascertain fluid intake and exclude other problems such as ill-fitting dentures or constipation.	Is the food provided suitable for elderly patients at all times of the day? Is the general pattern of meal-times appropriate? Do other patients complain about the menu? Are patients hurried	Patient continues to have indigestion in spite of adjustment in diet and reassessment of meal-times. Now complains at other times of the day. Reassessment of the situation is required with medical help.

Idealism or practical proposition?

Many nurses have been discouraged from adopting the nursing process because it is considered to be an 'American idea' which 'British nurses are doing anyway.' The term 'Nursing Process' itself has been a major deterrent and there are many misconceptions about what is actually entailed. Sometimes one part of the procedure, such as the assessment, has been instituted in the belief that this is all that is required.

The nursing process is a vehicle for making the philosophy of individually planned nursing care a reality. This belief is the foundation, and without it, implementation will not succeed.

There is a danger that poorly implemented schemes will cause the concepts of this systematic approach to nursing to come into disrepute, and consequently attempts to make this the basis of patient care will fail. Changes in attitude and thinking cannot be made in isolation, nor by a policy issued by nursing management. The principles may be taught in the School of Nursing, but the practice and development of ideas can only be implemented at the patient's side.

The first step is to assess the degree to which nurses are allocated to look after their own patients. This must be the short term aim, and the priority. The adoption of the nursing process can only be made when this is established, and time is required for nurses to assimilate the implications of this change from task assignment.

The merits of allocating nurses to a group of patients has been well documented[3] but there has been a slow response to introducing this — usually on the grounds that it requires more nurses. This is often more of an excuse than a reason. What is really needed is an attitude of mind which gives priority to wider dimensions of nursing care, those which extend beyond the actual giving of treatment and the performance of procedures.

No way has yet been found of measuring the ideal make-up of a ward or community team in terms of numbers and/or qualifications. It may be that this is not possible because of the diversity of patient dependency in terms of emotional as well as physical support. However, whilst recognising the lack of consistency in levels of staffing, it is often possible to form a small nursing team which can have the responsibility for certain patients. The important factor is that these patients can identify with a group of nurses, and with one nurse as particularly 'their own', throughout their stay in hospital. Continuity of nursing care is vital, not only for the patient's well-being, but in order that nurses can be truly accountable for all the stages of the nursing process, as they relate to 'their' patients. The rest of the team provide support and help to evaluate the care which is given. This will sometimes be a group of nurses obtaining clinical experience, especially when the number of qualified staff is limited. However, unless there are student nurses who are nearing the end of their training period, the assessment and planning of care should be the responsibility of a qualified nurse. Nurses have to learn these skills but should not take the ultimate decisions until they are state registered, and feel confident. It is important once the care plan has been made, that it is not altered when the nurse who constructed it is off-duty, unless the patient's condition changes, or new information necessitates a re-appraisal.

There will be situations where insufficient numbers of trained staff mean that the sister or nurse-in-charge must act as team leader. However, this is not ideal, and the rôle of the sister as supervisor and co-ordinator of the work of the staff nurses and enrolled nurses requires more emphasis. Once these nurses have assumed their responsibilities as team leaders, the sister is relieved of the constant interruptions which fragment her period of duty and make it less productive. A new art has to be learnt, that of delegation, combined with the ability to keep in touch. Fears that the nurse-in-charge will lose control are unfounded providing the channels of communication are open and effective.

When introducing the principles of the nursing process, a supportive nursing administration is essential and nurse managers must be seen to be knowledgeable concerning the theory and the philosophy entailed. They must also understand the constraints within each area. Just as the nursing team at ward or community level cannot act independently, neither can nursing management. There has to be a combined, carefully co-ordinated programme which also includes the contribution which will be made by members of the School of Nursing. It may be advantageous to have one person to act as this co-ordinator who is supported by a steering committee which has clearly defined terms of reference.

It is totally inadequate to arrange only one study day to initiate the staff. Several periods of instruction will be required, supplemented by workshops, relevant literature, and possibly visits to other areas where progress has already been made in implementing the nursing process. Sharing knowledge and experience can be of great value; at the moment there appears to be a tendency to implement schemes in isolation, even within one health authority.[4]

Nursing is in a state of transition, passing through an adolescent phase on the way to maturity. Sometimes it has seemed safer to cling to those elements which are well-known and tested, rather than take a risk and accept new methods. However it is evident that the majority of nurses are well aware of the need to reconsider methods of nursing practice. Unfortunately many good ideas are held back, and even abandoned, because there is a feeling that it is not worthwhile bringing them forward. What is more, it is often not long before these same nurses who wanted to institute change, adopt the attitudes of their senior colleagues. In this way the *status quo* is accepted as inevitable.

The challenge is to keep idealism alive. It is still as apparent as in the early years of nursing history. Most nurses speak of their desire to help people, and they see this as the way in which they will obtain fulfilment in their nursing. The search for this fulfilment must be satisfied. The principles underlying the nursing process provide one way in which this can happen.

References

1   Langham-Brown, S. J. 1981. Problems of patient care. *Nursing Times*, 11 June.

2   Nightingale, F. 1859. *Notes on Nursing: What it is and What it is not*, Chapter 13. Editions include Blackie, Glasgow, 1974; Dover, London, 1970 (paperback); Duckworth, London, 1970 (facsimile).

3   Matthews, A. 1982. 'Day-to-day organisation in the ward.' Chapter 5 in *In Charge of the Ward*. Oxford: Blackwell Scientific.

4   Norton, D. 1981. The nursing process in action. 1 – The quiet revolution: introduction of the nursing process in a region. *Nursing Times*, 17 June.

4

Setting and Controlling Standards

What is meant by a standard?

In many of the world's churches, there are chapels dedicated to members of the armed forces in which may be found their colours or standards. These are recognised by each regiment as the known symbol to follow. Within the nurse's job description there is usually a reference to maintaining standards. What this actually means is seldom stated. It is important in nursing to have a known symbol to follow as in any other organisation, so that professional values can be indentified. There is also the need to maintain standards of performance, and this cannot be done unless there is a means of measurement.

A standard is a fixed basis for comparison. It provides a criterion for what is best at a given time. Some standards may remain the same, but some will change with circumstances and the passage of time. With each generation, there comes the cry that standards are falling, not only in nursing, but in every aspect of daily life. Much depends upon the measure against which the criticised standard is being set and whether or not present norms have been considered. Methods may change, but certain principles will remain constant. It may no longer be considered necessary for a nurse to perform a blanket bath following a rigid procedure, as in the past, but rather that the method should be adapted to suit the individual patient and aimed at allowing his optimum participation. However, the needs for the water to be the correct temperature and for the patient's privacy, modesty and warmth to be preserved are essentials which will never change.

The criterion for excellence in nursing may be considered to be in assisting the patient in a way that will enable him to reach the fullest quality of life which is attainable and can be sustained. The International Council of Nurses' definition of nursing summarises this as follows:

> The fundamental responsibility of the nurse is to create an environment conducive to the physical, social and spiritual well-being to the greatest extent possible in the circumstances.

It is the element of creativeness and freedom to make decisions which ensures that a certain standard may still be maintained in differing situations.

Setting standards

What is essential, is that there should be some form of quality control as well as a control of quantity. For example, a falling waiting list of patients requiring surgery is not necessarily an indication that a higher standard of care is being reached when a 'conveyor belt' system of patient care may have developed. The priorities for nursing care must therefore be made known and the meaning of nursing of quality has to be clearly spelt out, so that it is obvious to all concerned when this is not being achieved or maintained. It is necessary that nurses have the ability, and the confidence, to speak out in support of their beliefs in a logical and unemotional way and can give strength to their arguments by sound knowledge and firm facts. It is not too difficult to measure falling standards of physical care, but it is not easy when considering some of the other aspects of care; for instance, to ensure that there is sufficient time for the nurse to talk and listen to patients and prepare them adequately for their various ordeals.

Nurses rarely work in isolation; personal standards will therefore be seen within the framework of the overall objectives of the organisation or wherever care is taking place. The standards of an organisation will be formed as a combination of its philosophy, policies and procedures, together with the ethical code, to serve one ultimate purpose, namely, the provision of the highest possible quality of care. An organisation may also be an educational institution, with the additional responsibility of providing the opportunity and facilities for the acquisition of skills and knowledge. Certain standards will then be expected by authorities outside the organisation itself.

There must be mutually agreed standards and codes of practice to ensure the safety of the patient and to protect the nurse within the sphere of work.

The essential framework in reaching an agreement for the desired standards may be seen to be:

(a) The nurses at every level share in the decisions regarding all factors, so that they are acceptable.

(b) That when agreed they should be written down and communicated to all members of the health care team. This is essential since a policy designed to determine a certain standard for one group will often affect the work of others.

(c)   That they are capable of being interpreted in the working environment and that there is a system of control which ensures that what is agreed actually happens.

(d)   That they are revised as circumstances change.

The balance between the desirable and the possible

In determining the priorities of care, it is necessary to have complete agreement regarding the minimum level at which standards should be maintained. This not only ensures that the quality is compatible with the beliefs of those giving care, but also considers the rights of the recipients and provides security and safety for all involved.

If nurses feel that the provision and maintenance of a certain standard of care is impossible, there is the danger that morale within the organisation will fall as job satisfaction is difficult to achieve. As a result, there is a build up of tension and frustration which adversely affects the working environment and standards fall even lower. Therefore, it is important that the expectations of each member of the team are discussed to be sure that they are realistic and compatible with the resources available.

The factors to be considered are:

The people involved
- Numbers
- Qualifications/training/experience
- Interaction between workers — 'team spirit'
- Personal philosophies
- Commitment for providing learning opportunities
- Supporting services and quality of liaison

The environment
- Space/design
- Facilities for patients and staff
- Lighting, heating etc

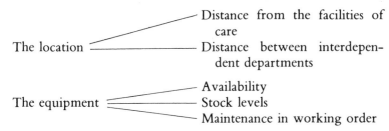

The location
— Distance from the facilities of care
— Distance between interdependent departments

The equipment
— Availability
— Stock levels
— Maintenance in working order

It is important to come to terms with the fact that excellence in all situations, at all times, is difficult, if not impossible. It is equally important not to become complacent that standards of care are at a satisfactory level and not to deny that there is room for improvement. There is a need to scrutinise regularly what is being done, to exclude the unnecessary. Circumstances are never such that they cannot be improved.

A balance therefore has to be found between what is possible and what is essential. For example:

BALANCE

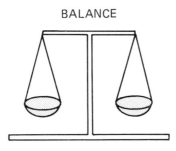

POSSIBLE	ESSENTIAL
The development of a personal relationship. The allocation of one nurse to be responsible for assessing, planning, implementing and evaluating the care of the patient.	The allocation of the care of the patient to someone who is competent and equipped for the task.
That the time schedule is geared to the patient's individual requirements.	That drugs and treatments are given on time. That there is a pattern to the day which allows for rest, sleep, food and comfort.
That the patient is helped to reach the optimum quality of life.	That short term and, it is hoped, some long term goals are reached.

Measuring standards of care

The measurement of standards of care may be difficult because it is relative to the perceptions and attitudes of the individuals involved. This is not to say that it is impossible. An attempt must be made.

Assessing performance

Some aspects of nursing care are more easily assessed than others, the most obvious being the skills and techniques involved in giving direct care to patients. A ward sister or charge nurse may observe a nurse doing a patient's wound dressing and may consider that a safe standard has not been achieved because all the principles of asepsis have not been practised. This is easily measured against known principles. In addition, there is usually a standard procedure agreed by the organisation and contained in a Procedure Manual. The failure of many nursing procedure books however often lies in the fact that they only provide guidance to how a task is performed without mention of the aims and supporting principles. (See also Chapter 2 page 14.)

The assessment of performance is to a certain extent dependent upon the attitudes and personal standards of the assessor. It is therefore necessary to identify the standards required in the provision of all the aspects of patient care and to establish criteria for measurement and monitoring. It also has to be decided who will be responsible for making these decisions so that the principles can apply to all situations and be put into practice.

The areas of care which are more difficult to assess, and yet are inseparable from any aspect of patient care, including the most highly technical tasks, are the interpersonal skills required in building up the relationship between nurse and patient; the skills required to ensure that a patient's needs have been accurately assessed and effectively met. The difficulty arises not only because the observer can only make a subjective measurement of good interaction between two people, but because nurses have not yet become accustomed to acknowledging the need to acquire and develop these skills. By such acknowledgement, the imperfections in providing true total care for patients can be highlighted and then, as knowledge is gained with experience, the development of criteria for the evaluation of indirect nursing care may be aided (Fig. 3.1).

Staff appraisal

This allows an opportunity for a formal review of the areas of accountability, and for constructive discussion of the nurse's performance. However, it does not directly develop criteria for measuring standards of nursing care, nor does the present national staff appraisal form provide sufficient material for setting objectives in relation to personal standards.

It is possible to prepare a comprehensive appraisal document which goes a long way towards this by identifying the key areas in which the nurse fulfils his or her role and is accountable. The standard which is expected of the nurse can then be outlined alongside it. For example, in relation to the role and function of the staff nurse, one of the items would read:

Key Area *Group Leadership*	*Standard of Performance* *to be achieved*
1 Provides an environment conducive to good work where there is mutual trust and a happy atmosphere.	Is able to obtain a satisfactory response from patients and others by means of interpersonal skills, and can promote effective teamwork.

Nursing audit, quality control

Several methods of nursing audit are being developed, notably in North America. Evidence of all aspects of the nursing process is sought, either retrospectively by examining patients' charts and records, or concurrently, by random visits of appointed auditors to observe the care actually being delivered to certain patients.

Retrospective chart audit may not be considered entirely satisfactory, for although lessons may be learnt which may improve care in the future, it has little bearing on the actual care given at the time of its delivery. A nurse may produce a beautiful chart, a work of art with every dot and cross carefully coloured and recorded religiously at. stated times, but the patient may not have been comfortable. Likewise, a nurse's written record of a patient's stay in a ward may give an incomplete picture of the care actually given. For example, a staff nurse recorded that one of her patients had been 'nursed sitting well up the bed'. In fact, the patient had constantly slipped down the bed and the nurses' ingenuity was stretched to find ways of preventing this. No mention of the problems encountered, of the methods tried or of their subsequent failure was actually recorded. Concurrent audit, made whilst the patient is actually receiving care, provides an opportunity to correct any unsatisfactory conditions there and then.

In the long term, either method should reveal deficiencies which can be corrected, by highlighting the reasons for their occurrence. It also identifies staff who may need further training or up-dating and therefore may enhance the maintenance of standards in this way.

It is significant that doctors as well as nurses are considering these methods as a means of controlling standards, and that much discussion is currently being directed to the question of medical audit.

Self-assessment

It may be considered that the most appropriate type of audit, in the pursuit of maintaining high standards, is that of self-assessment, that is, constantly reviewing one's own performance in relation to the philosophy held. Although this should always be done, there is also a need for the stimulation to do better, and the recognition of success in order to give encouragement. The observations of others, especially one's peers, can reveal the 'blind spots', which every individual has to their own attitudes and behaviour. If criticism is constructive and given with kindness and concern, there is opportunity for mutual benefit.

Patient satisfaction

The person who can best assess the appropriateness and effectiveness of the care given is the patient. Some health care systems, again mainly in North America, have attempted this method, using questionnaires or interview techniques. The reliability of this method may be questioned, as patients are on the whole very reluctant to make even constructive criticisms of their own care. They may feel that any discomfort experienced during a period of ill health is either part of the whole unpleasant business or that it will only have to be endured for a short time until normal life may be resumed. The criticism which is made tends therefore to be retrospective and, although enquiry into a patient's adverse comments may help improve standards for the future, it will not have an effect on the care they actually received. However, this is an area which may be considered worthy of further study.

Measurement against objectives

Unless some criterion is established, evaluation of care and decisions about nursing standards will remain vague. An effective means of assessing standards may be found by systematic recording of the nursing process. Desired standards should be synonymous with the objectives stated in the patient's plan of care. If all the factors have been taken into account and the goals considered realistic, this forms a minimum and attainable standard. If the goals are found to be unrealistic, the areas which are unsatisfactory can be identified, together with the reasons for their existence. This is well illustrated in a published nursing care plan. [1]

A man had been admitted to hospital following a fall from scaffolding and had required surgery to evacuate an extradural haematoma. When he was admitted to the ward, the nurse noted, as part of her assessment of his needs for care, that the patient was unable to move any part of his body except for the rare movement of his left arm and leg. He was unable to support his back and limbs. She saw this as a problem and realised that there was a risk that his joints would stiffen. Her goal was that the limb joints should not stiffen during the period of immobility and that they would retain the normal range of motion. Her plan of care was to perform the full range of movement exercises at two hourly intervals. When the care was evaluated, it was noted that even though the patient was still unable to move himself, the plan had not been implemented every two hours 'because of staff shortage'. Although physiotherapy involved passive exercises, the limb joints, especially the upper ones, were stiff.

In the above example, it is clearly shown that because care had not been given at the frequency assessed as necessary, the patient's physical condition had not been maintained and had in fact deteriorated. The nurse had stated honestly that the care which had been prescribed had not been given. Therefore the objective had not been achieved, not because of an inaccurate assessment of the need or the required frequency of care to meet it, but because of the lack of the necessary resources.

So often nurses are reluctant to state that the care they wish to give is not being achieved. Stated objectives which have been unfulfilled are sound proof that the quality of care is not of the standard desired and expected. This then provides a strong weapon in any argument for an increase of necessary resources. Nursing care plans therefore may provide a greater indication of the standards being aimed at and which are actually possible. These will be stated in terms of quality rather than quantity (see p. 29), something which workload and nurse—patient dependency studies fail to do, since these concentrate on the analysis of tasks.

It is *not* impossible to measure standards of care. The stumbling block comes when necessary action is not taken when care falls below what has been identified as the minimum standard. Nurses in particular have always been expected to cope with any situation, rather than to insist that care cannot be given to the accepted standard. Perhaps this is because to do so is seen as an admission of failure, rather than an honest appraisal of an impossible situation.

Accountability and responsibility

As nursing develops an increasing professional autonomy, areas of accountability will be more readily recognised and defined. These areas of care will be those for which the nurse accepts responsibility and may then be held as accountable for how care is given and for whether or not the accepted standard has been achieved.

As members of a profession, nurses should be striving for standards of excellence and assuming a personal responsibility for adding their contribution toward improving care. Since the situation in which the work is done is always changing, there is an obligation to be aware of current and fresh ideas and to welcome new methods of giving, assessing and measuring care.

Reference

1   Houlton, E. 1978. Rediscovering the patient. *Nursing Times Supplement*, 30 November, pp. 8–13.

5
The Nurse and the Doctor — a Partnership?

Conflict in Change

As nurses strive to identify their unique role in the care of a patient, conflict may arise between medical and nursing staff. This is often because of misunderstanding of the many changes which have influenced the role of the nurse in recent years. Indeed, nurses themselves have sometimes found it difficult to demonstrate to their medical colleagues the advantages of sharing decisions on an equal basis. It may be that nurses have not truly understood the meaning and effect of the autonomy they seek, and that this has tended to alienate them from the other health workers.

Nursing has followed a pattern which was originally defined by doctors, and this trend has continued. It must be acknowledged that although this meant that nursing was founded on the medical model, there were advantages, not only in the development of ethics and standards, but in the willingness of doctors to participate in nurse training in the School of Nursing and in the wards. It has however been partly responsible for the relationship seen between the doctor and nurse as that of leader and follower.

As the position of women in society changes this will be reflected in nursing especially in a situation where women are still overwhelmingly in the majority. This factor, together with other developments which necessitate fresh thinking about the nature and the function of nursing, will have implications within the health care team. Many doctors and nurses saw the recommendations of the Salmon Committee[1] as the beginning of a change in the relationship between them. However, criticism aimed at the new structure often failed to recognise that the old system was no longer viable, nor appropriate, for meeting the demands which would be made on nurses in the future. It is clear that failure in this instance to discuss fully the implications with all who would be involved, produced misconceptions. Nurses themselves were unsure of their new roles and therefore found it difficult to explain their function to others. There must be complete understanding between the two professions of their respective aims and objectives if there is to be an effective working partnership. This is true at national level also, and it is suggested that there has been a deterioration in the image of the nurse as a decision-maker within the World Health Organisation:[2]

> The natural tendency was for the physician to turn to the nurse because he saw her as a partner or co-worker. Now he turns to the psychologist, sociologist, economist or lawyer. Of course these people have a place, but if you don't sort out the relationships within the direct care provider team, then you are in real trouble.

Discussion and making decisions

Medical and nursing objectives are complementary but they are not interchangeable. Any change, therefore, no matter how small, within medical and nursing thinking will affect each discipline. For example, increased medical knowledge may demand greater technical skill on the part of the nurse, which may involve the use of specialised equipment, adding to the total care required by a patient. In order to ensure that the patient receives adequate nursing and medical care, it is essential that the implications are discussed and the care needs planned together. It may need only a reorganisation of nursing staff, but it may require extra resources.

Likewise, when a ward sister wishes to try a new system of ward management or implement a policy that she feels is important to the comfort and well-being of her patients, her decision cannot be made in isolation. For example, in the introduction of a period during the day when provision is made for the patients to rest, consideration needs to be given to ensure that the time chosen is the most appropriate for all concerned. The reasons why the ward should be 'closed' during this time, except in exceptional circumstances, need to be made clear.

The perennial problem of planning the use of beds in a hospital ward might be eased in a similar way, the doctor and nurse in charge together constantly reviewing the actual with the anticipated workload in relation to standards of patient care. Medical and nursing aims must be united; this may be clearly seen in decisions related to readiness of a patient for discharge. The medical objectives of successful recovery from a surgical procedure may be achieved before the nursing objective, which entails restoring the patient to his previous ability to care for himself; therefore planning potential discharge dates together is essential. In an increasingly demanding day, it must not be forgotten that a quiet time in which to discuss such matters, on a regular basis, is part of the means to fulfilling the responsibility to provide quality care — time spent sharing a coffee- or tea-time should be seen as being as valuable as that spent on the ward round making purely clinical decisions.

These principles seem commonsense, and yet, they do not always happen. Nurses and doctors are taught to show empathy toward their patients; this should extend to each other to enable them to give mutual support in sharing problems and to show an increased understanding of difficulties.

Opportunities for shared education

One way in which a closer understanding of the distinct function of doctors and nurses may be acquired is by shared learning. For example, there is a project in a London teaching group to provide teaching in the care of the elderly on a multidisciplinary basis, involving medical, physiotherapy and nursing students.[3] Lectures are shared, and also seminars, case conferences and clinical practice. It may also be considered that as higher educational requirements for nursing are acknowledged and there is a move toward an educational experience rather than a training, the gap between the groups of 'carers' may narrow.

So many of the subjects related to patient care, particularly in the social sciences, are not the prerogative of just one of the caring professions. The assessment of a patient's needs for nursing care and the making of a medical diagnosis, require the same interpersonal and observational skills. If these principles were taught to all students together, on a theoretical basis, there seems no reason why this cannot continue in practice. The nurse may be acting as the doctor's assistant, but will also be picking up cues for her own assessment of the patient's needs. Often the same question is asked by a number of people, or a procedure such as the estimation of blood-pressure will be repeated by the doctor as well as the nurse. The information gained may be the same, but the use made of it will be different when formulating the medical and nursing plan. A joint approach will be appreciated by the patient and will be less tiring.

Re-examination of the methods used for recording both by doctors and nurses is required. This applies to both their assessments and their subsequent plans. Projects have begun in North America and Scandinavia to explore the possibility of joint records. This would imply mutual trust and truly shared objectives to ensure that both plans are compatible and in the patient's best interest.

Shared concepts

The hospice movement is an excellent example of how doctors and nurses can look together at the *actual* needs of people, and accept that the emphasis can, and must, change to give prestige to caring as well as curing.

From a patient's point of view, much of the suffering which doctors and nurses should be alleviating is not only in the areas of acute illness. For positive attitudes towards maintaining health to be realised, there must be agreement between the professions, and the doctor and nurse must strive to achieve this together.

References

1   *Report of the Committee on the Senior Nursing Staff Structure* (Salmon Report). 1966. London: HMSO.
2   Larger than life. Interview with Dorothy Hall, Regional Nursing Officer, WHO, Copenhagen. 1981. *Nursing Times*, 4 June.
3   Hutt, A. 1980. Shared learning for shared care: Multi-disciplinary course at the Middlesex Hospital. *Journal of Advanced Nursing*, July (Vol. 5, No. 4), pp. 389–394.

6

Applying the Nursing Ethic

Responsibility and decisions

With every privilege there is a responsibility, and the freedom to make decisions is a privilege. The willingness to consider the results of a course of action, and to assume accountability for the outcome, must therefore accompany the decision.

To exercise responsibility a person has to 'respond' to situations as they occur. Where nurses are concerned this invariably involves them with people. Nurses have not only to consider all the facts which pertain to those situations, but also the further dimension of the ethical implications. Let us suppose the nurse is participating in the care of a patient receiving behaviour therapy in a psychiatric hospital. A certain regime may be established which deprives the patient of the ordinary comforts of daily living as well as visits from friends and family. These are used as rewards to produce compliance and good behaviour.[1] It could be asked whether such treatment is ethical, that is whether the patient's rights are respected. It is difficult to decide what is right in these circumstances, and it would be easy to lay the responsibility elsewhere, with the psychiatrist or the psychologist. However, to disregard the issue is to fail in fulfilling the obligations of the professional nurse to the patient.

There are two criteria which can be used when faced with complex decisions. The first is to apply the principle to oneself, and consider if what is being asked of the patient would be acceptable personally in a similar situation. The second is to remember that people should be treated as ends in themselves, and not as a means to an end. In the light of these criteria it could be argued that the incident described is failing to satisfy ethical considerations.

The responsible person has to be prepared to stand firm when others disagree. There must also be the ability to state a case, and defend a judgement should this be challenged. This is often acquired only as the result of experience gained the hard way. Margaret Cooper, Chief Education Officer of the General Nursing Council put it this way:[2]

In so far as we live for others, we do so not only by our actions and attitudes, but also by our interior state, what we are, and what we

41

experience most deeply inside us; the happiness and misery which come to us, the exulting and the agony we experience as individuals alone. But they are not for us alone. They are for mankind.

Motivation and decisions

No amount of intensity of feeling can be a substitute for clarity of thought, and sometimes it may be necessary to control strong emotions in order to be objective. Clear thinking begins with a self–examination of the motive underlying a decision. When treatment which has little prospect of helping a patient is continued after the stage when recovery is unlikely, the motive could be questioned. Is it to reassure nurse and doctor that they are still taking positive measures, even if cure is impossible? Or is it to convince the relatives that active steps are still being taken? If the latter, it is clearly wrong to give false hopes, for the relatives will be unprepared for the loss of a member of the family.

From this example it is clear that a failure to study personal motives can influence the nursing objectives, and also the nursing plan. It can also produce much inner conflict and concern among nurses who would prefer to concentrate on sustaining the patient and giving all possible comfort at this time. The freedom to choose and apply motives is a heavy responsibility which doctors, nurses and members of the health professions all share, and it is essential that this combined motivation is compatible with the ultimate good of those receiving their care.

A common basis for questioning

A simple solution toward solving ethical matters might appear to be the establishment of a District Ethical Committee to whom all questions could be referred, and thus relieve the individual of responsibility. There is no doubt that such a Committee is essential and this is emphasised in Chapter 7 which discusses the nurse's response to advances in technology. Representation on the Committee must include nurses, but there are other members of the caring team, such as physiotherapists who have to consider the ethical implications of what they do. Invariably it is a question of teamwork, particularly where research projects are concerned. The nurse's part in relating ethics to research will be discussed later.

Guidelines are needed which can be used by all the health service professionals so that there is common ground for evaluating a proposal. In this way there would be less likelihood of the trauma which can occur when a course of action is unacceptable to a particular member of the team.

A pattern which would meet this need has been prepared by Brian Bliss and Alan Johnson in their book, *Aims and Motives in Clinical Medicine.*[3] They suggest a kind of 'ethical identification key' based on a series of questions.

There are two preliminary activities: firstly, defining precisely what is involved. Words can mean various things to different people, and there must be a common understanding of the terms used. Secondly, there must be a positive effort to avoid the danger of making comparisons between dissimilar factors. For example, if it is suggested that there should be no hesitation in terminating pregnancy because it is as accidental as contracting venereal disease, which no one would refuse to treat, this equates the killing of a human foetus with the destruction of bacteria.

The main questions which constitute the guidelines are as follows:

1 What are the AIMS — are these right or wrong?
2 Is the METHOD to achieve the aims right or wrong?
3 Are the long-term results and the incidental effects of the proposal right or wrong? What are the RESULTS?

Study of these questions makes it clear that members of the health professions should be getting together more frequently to discuss current issues and apply these questions. Only in this way can they test their reactions and recognise what their conscience tells them is right. Subjects such as new techniques in the field of genetics, or the controversy surrounding voluntary euthanasia require attention. It only takes very minor changes in ethical values for practices previously unacceptable to become the norm.

Nurses must take the initiative together with medical colleagues. Often seminars are arranged for medical and nursing students, but there are few opportunities for combined discussion after qualifying. It is not always necessary to make formal arrangements, the situations which raise ethical issues are more likely to arise during the course of everyday work. Lack of time cannot be an excuse for neglecting these matters, they have to assume much more significance if decisions are to be made in the true interest of patients.

Legal issues and the nursing ethic

Reference should be made to literature prepared by experts for guidance on the relationship between nursing ethics and legal requirements. However, it may be helpful to give just two examples which show the importance of these matters.

The first example concerns the code of practice which has been prepared by a working party on behalf of the Health Departments regarding the Removal of Cadaveric Organs for transplantation.[4] Knowledge of the code cannot be neglected because nurses consider this to be solely the province of those working in transplantation centres. It is essential information for all nurses if the donor's wishes are to be respected, and if these have not been expressed, to ensure that relatives, who may have objections, feel that their views have been taken into account. Such matters as retaining the anonymity of the donor and recipient are clearly stated in the Code, so that distress is not caused to the family of the donor or to the recipient, by involvement of the media.

The Code of Practice includes a sample check list to make sure that the administrative and legal requirements have been fulfilled. There is also a clinical check list to secure certainty of the diagnosis of 'Brain Death'. It has recently been decided that these checks shall be done twice, and that two consultants shall be involved in the decision-making. However, whilst such matters are a medical responsibility, nurses must be aware of the conclusions of the conference of the Royal Colleges of Medicine[5] which clarify the irreversible state which constitutes death, and keep themselves informed of any amendments or revision of the criteria which may be accepted as necessary in the light of experience.

The second example refers to staff shortages. There is obviously a reluctance on the part of nurses to restrict the services they give to the public who need them. However the prime responsibility is to give *safe* care. If in the opinion of the nurse the situation is unsafe, there is an ethical duty to make this known to those in authority. If a mistake occurs when the appropriately trained staff are not available and other nurses assume duties for which they are not properly prepared, there are likely to be legal problems which could involve the nurses concerned. They have a personal responsibility not to undertake such tasks unless there is a real emergency.

It follows that if a nurse delegates a responsibility to those who are not equipped to do the job and a mistake is made, the delegating nurse stands accountable. This raises the question of duties under-taken by nursing auxiliaries. Even if they have attended a course of instruction, they do not receive the theoretical teaching given in the educational programme for enrolment or state registration. The auxiliary therefore is unlikely to understand the reasons behind a physiological or psychological response when caring for a patient. The fact that considerable practical experience has been built up over a long period is no safeguard. In spite of the attention given to this subject in the Report of the Committee on Nursing[6] there is much confusion about the limits and the extent of the responsibilities of auxiliary personnel. This problem has to be solved, for the qualified nurse has a duty to ensure that their function is defined, and then that the requisite training is given.

Telling the truth

Nurses are aware of the importance of integrity in their professional life. It implies wholeness and self respect, which in turn create a respect for the dignity and worth of all human beings. Integrity also includes trust and adherence to the truth. The patient relies on the nurse to establish a trusting relationship so that information can be given in confidence and with the sure knowledge that it will not be divulged. This is illustrated in the following episode. The patient was only 29 years old. She had been admitted to the ward several times having taken an overdose of drugs. She was also an alcoholic. Her husband had tried to help by ensuring his wife had no access to alcohol and just enough money for the housekeeping. The patient's mother did not know of her daughter's problem, and unfortunately every time the daughter attempted to take her life the mother blamed her son-in-law. One evening the husband shared this problem with the Staff Nurse, asking her to keep the information in confidence. Shortly afterwards the patient was discharged home. Three weeks later the patient was readmitted, and Staff Nurse noticed that the husband was very depressed and looking ill and tired. Knowing the probable reason for his deterioration in health she felt she should seek help for him. However, having been given the information about his domestic affairs in confidence, she could only encourage him to seek advice and ask the health visitor to call as a routine visit.

If this relationship of trust is to be maintained it is essential that both doctor and nurse decide together what to tell patients and their families, particularly when the prognosis is not good. The truth given with compassion, can often be a relief. The so-called 'white lie' will only suffice for a time, and meanwhile the burden of doubt may have been carried by the patient or his family causing much distress and unspoken fear. There is always a time which is right for open discussion about what is happening. The observant nurse will know when the right moment has come, and also how much the patient and the family can bear at that time. What is essential is that those caring for the patient are in agreement about what is said, and are there to give support afterwards. It is often the gradual realisation of the truth over the next few hours or days which is hard to accept and during this time the patient or relative can feel very much alone.

The duty to tell the truth is not always so apparent when problems arise which concern professional colleagues. Loyalty to a friend whose judgement is impaired because of misappropriation of drugs may deter a nurse from making this known to nursing management. However, if there has been a genuine attempt to persuade the friend to seek help and this does not happen, the nurse has to consider patients and clients who may be at risk. The good of the public must have precedence. The nurse also has an obligation to the friend who is jeopardising future prospects. This is an offence which has to be investigated by the General Nursing Council in the interest of protecting the public and maintaining professional standards. It is also possible that the friend is needing specialist help which can be more readily obtained once the circumstances are made known to the authorities.

Ethics and research

It is important that all nurses are familiar with the ethical implications of research projects. Application of the three questions outlined on p. 43 makes a good starting point. This will ensure scrutiny of the aims, the methods and the results of what is done, and make sure that what is best and right for the individuals who will be involved is kept constantly in mind.

Useful guidance is given in a small booklet entitled *Ethics Related to Research in Nursing*,[7] and this is essential reading for any nurse doing research, even in its simplest form. Reminders are given about the patient's consent, the use of data, confidentiality, and the protection of the patient from harm during the proceedings. It is essential that in obtaining the patient's consent, that he or she truly understands the implications, and that there is the right of refusal. Sometimes patients may find it difficult to decline, and in these situations the nurse responsible can help the patient to come to a decision by answering queries which may arise.

An aspect of research which often causes concern to nurses is the giving of placebos. Most problems arise because patients have not been given an adequate and honest explanation of the trial in terms which safeguard the relationship between doctor, nurse and patient. Nurses can use their influence to make sure that such explanations do take place and that patients truly understand and wish to co-operate.

It is unfortunate that few nursing manuals contain guidance for nurses who may be asked to participate in a clinical trial by medical staff. This should be remedied in order to make sure that research activities do not occupy a disproportionate amount of the nurse's time and consequently have an adverse effect on nursing care.

Guidance is also necessary to protect the nurse who may be asked to be a volunteer in a clinical trial, so that discretion and good sense prevail, especially if there is any question that there may be a temporary physical incapacity, however slight.

It is helpful to warn nurses of the implications of participating in data collection methods associated with the advertising of a particular product. This is ethically unacceptable, since it could be misconstrued as a form of self-advertisement.

The values of society

No chapter about the nursing ethic would be complete without reference to the conflict that can arise when the values held by society are not in accordance with those of professional nurses. Most people would not think it wrong to do another job on a rest day in order to obtain extra money for the family budget. The professional nurse, however, has to consider that over-tiredness precipitates errors of judgement which could be harmful to patients. The use of leisure to avoid fatigue has a special significance.

In welcoming higher standards of living, society has come to rely on material comforts as a right, not necessarily earned; and this has had an effect on attitudes toward work. As a result it may be difficult sometimes for friends and relatives to understand that nurses have to work unsocial hours and honour commitments over and above their normal duty times.

Changing codes of behaviour have meant that nurses sometimes require help and explanation before they can accept a professional code which has previously been unchallenged. The touch of the nurse's hand as an expression of understanding which can mean so much to a patient, may have other connotations for the new entrant to nursing. Unless the use of touch is explained in professional terms rather than the sexual and social context, this form of communication may be avoided by nurses and a vital means of human contact will be denied to patients.

Whilst the ethics of any profession must be reviewed in the light of sociological change, there are basic principles common to all the caring professions which cannot change. The most important of these have been identified in this chapter, but there will be other fundamental questions which require careful thought. It is the responsibility of experienced nurses to help colleagues to come to grips with some of the ethical dilemmas which they will meet in the course of their work. This is done by making opportunities to think through the issues and not by imposing a particular point of view. In this way, attitudes, beliefs and values can be articulated and put to the test, and standards of personal morality can be examined alongside those required by the profession.

References

1   Macmillan, P. 1979. Let the punishment fit the crime? *Nursing Times*, 29 September.
2   Cooper, M. J. P. 1974. 'Attitudes and values in nursing education.' Paper given at a conference on 'Wider Issues in Nursing Education', Queen's College, Birmingham, 4–6 January. (Selected conference papers published by The Institute of Religion and Medicine.)
3   Bliss, B. P. and Johnson, A. G. 1975. *Aims and Motives in Clinical Medicine*. London: Pitman Medical.
4   *Code of Practice on the Removal of Cadaveric Organs for Transplantation*. 1980. London: DHSS.
5   Memorandum on the diagnosis of death. 1976. *British Medical Journal*, Vol. 2, pp. 1187–1188.
6   *Report of the Committee on Nursing* (Briggs Report). 1972. London: HMSO.
7   *Ethics Related to Research in Nursing*. 1977. London: Rcn.

7

The Nurse and Technology

Useful tool or stumbling block?

Technology has been described as organised knowledge applied to practical tasks. Since nursing embodies many such tasks, there must be a place for technology. Yet there is justifiable concern that the machine will take control, and that technical tasks will increasingly become status symbols to the detriment of nursing skills. Indeed if this were to happen, it would negate all the principles upon which nursing of quality is founded, and the role of the nurse as described in previous chapters would not be attainable. The more positive view is that technology should be a useful tool in the hands of nurses to enhance their work and enable them to take their place with other professionals who have applied new theories and methods to current practice.

It is wrong to stand in the way of progress, so some means has to be found of harnessing technical expertise to ensure that it is applied with wisdom and in safety. There is an urgent need to create a theory of nursing based on scientific evaluation of what is practised, but this cannot be done without considering the impact of technology on the work of the nurse. There are two options open, either nurses can allow technical innovations to supersede their caring role, or they can concentrate on meeting fundamental human needs of those in their care.

At the present time it is evident that many mothers in the United Kingdom feel strongly that they wish to have the right to decide whether they will have their baby delivered at home or in hospital. The Report on Perinatal and Neonatal Mortality[1] confirms that one of the reasons for this reaction is the use of sophisticated equipment in the process of delivery, and the institutional atmosphere of the labour ward. Suggestions are made to overcome such problems, but it cannot be denied that in this instance, the human needs of the mother, and the psychological support she requires, may be jeopardised in an effort to ensure access to life-saving equipment. The options are evident in the following question put by Robert Dingwall of the Research Centre for Socio-legal Studies, Oxford.[2]

Should nurses seek to resume patient contact tasks that they have relinquished? Alternatively, will nursing contract into a rather small occupation carrying out routine technical tasks, and supervising a semi-skilled auxiliary workforce?

Technology in action

The areas in which nurses can expect to find the impact of technology both now and in the future can be conveniently identified as follows:

1 Diagnostic purposes
2 The treatment of illness
3 Providing equipment and aids
4 Rehabilitation following illness or incapacity
5 Recording and storing information
6 Teaching and learning

Each area will be discussed briefly, showing through examples where the nurse can contribute to the application of technology. Unless there is a clear understanding of what is entailed, there is a danger that new techniques and equipment may appear so attractive that they are adopted without adequate study of the implications. It is part of the nurse's responsibility to see that technology is put to good use and for the patient's benefit.

1   *Diagnosis*

Sisters and charge nurses in Neurosurgical Units will be familiar with the ordeal of the patient when having an air encephalogram. Now it is possible with computerised axial tomography (EMI Scan) to make measurements by irradiation which give similar but more accurate information. For the patient this not only obviates a small surgical operation, but also the subsequent headache. Technology in this instance has not only improved the quality of the diagnostic material, but has saved the patient much discomfort. The apparatus is expensive, but so obviously beneficial that nurses can be confident in supporting the installation of the equipment.

There is a danger that the availability of sophisticated diagnostic apparatus could mean that medical and nursing staff lose faith in their own ability to observe and record physical signs. They may feel that mechanical confirmation must be sought routinely in order to be sure of a diagnosis. However, for the very sick patient this may entail an ordeal of another kind, namely an ambulance journey to another hospital where the special equipment is installed. Discretion is necessary to weigh up what is really best for the patient in the particular circumstances. Wherever additional resources are available, a balance has to be found between excessive use just because they are there, and what is actually needed.

2   Treatment

There are so many ways in which technology has contributed to the treatment of disease that it is difficult to single out one special instance. For nurses the advent of new techniques means the acquisition of fresh knowledge, learning new skills and a readiness to participate in some of the ethical decisions which may ensue. There is also the question of finance. Difficult decisions sometimes have to be made, such as limiting the expenditure on a new technique which will benefit a particular group of patients so that help can be given to a large number requiring treatment of a more routine nature.

This kind of dilemma is apparent when considering the treatment of patients who require haemodialysis. The materials used during treatment are costly, and many staff are required for a hospital unit. This raises the question of the location of the machine, and whether it is more economical to install this in the patient's home. For the patient this can mean saving journeys to hospital, and it may be possible to dialyse at night and so avoid having to take time off from work. On the other hand, experienced nurses must be available to supervise dialysis in the home, and to undertake the necessary teaching of the patient and relatives in the first instance. Nurses cannot ignore these financial issues, since with only a certain amount of money available, where it is spent will affect their work and the amount of specialised treatment which can be undertaken.

There are other matters to think about within the specialised unit, and these concern the extension of the role of the nurse beyond her normal function. In order that there can be continuity of care for the patient, it is inevitable that nurses do certain technical tasks which have previously been done by doctors. In accepting these duties, nurses have also to accept the full responsibility for their actions and make sure that they have received adequate instruction from a senior member of the medical staff in the first place. They must also have the backing of their employing authority. [3]

3   Equipment and Aids

Ripple beds, lifting aids and efficient nurse-call systems, are all examples of where technology has assisted nurses on the job. They have to be used efficiently and knowledgeable technicians must be available for regular servicing. Ripple beds are of little use without sufficient pillows to support the patient, and give comfort and good positioning. The patient is dependent on the nurse's ability to use such equipment intelligently. The application of the science of ergonomics has produced an assortment of furniture suitable for elderly people, so it is necessary to take the trouble to choose the right type of chair for the particular person.

Nurses are not sufficiently vocal in stating what they want to help them with their tasks. They have to initiate research and tell the technicians what is required. For example, simple devices such as the book rest with accompanying page turner can mean a great deal to the patient who is immobilised on his back.

4   Rehabilitation

Closed circuit television can be used to magnify print and pictures on a screen so that visually handicapped people can read and write. This kind of apparatus has been known to enable a librarian to go back to her books and an architect to his drawing desk. There are many opportunities for the technologist in helping the handicapped to lead more satisfying and independent lives. Nurses can contribute by knowing what is available and being ready to call on the technician where there is a specific problem.

Learning to live with a disability is a hard task, and it is often when the initial recovery from illness or accident has been accomplished that the testing time comes. This is when the nurse can do so much to give support and encouragement, and if necessary help the patient to overcome the fear of a machine or technical equipment. The aids which are available will be of little use unless the patient has the will to recover, and the nurse is the best person to understand when the patient is ready for mechanical aids, and what is the best time for an introduction to other professionals, such as the Occupational Therapist.

5   Recording and storing information

Information is much more freely shared in an age where communications are swift and conveyed visually as well as by the written and
spoken word. This means that maintaining confidentiality is
difficult. It is also a fact that society pays less attention to the need for
personal privacy than in the past.

The arrival of the computer has increased the possibilities for
linking information, and a committee under the chairmanship of
Sir Norman Lindop was constituted in 1978, to consider the
protection of individual rights in relation to the collection and
storage of personal data on computers. [4] This has significance for the
medical and nursing professions who may wish to use computers for
patient's records, for vaccination and immunisation programmes,
and for statistical information such as the incidence of non-
accidental injuries to children. The committee recommended a
Code of Practice to be drawn up by the Health Service Professions,
and the setting up of a Data Protection Authority. In some Health
Districts it is established that the implications of computerisation are
considered by the local Standing Ethical Committee, so that a Code
of Practice is available for all those likely to be concerned.

Nurses have to think carefully about access to nursing records,
and suggestions such as patients being able to see their own. It is
understood that medical records are the responsibility of the
Consultant, but the situation is less clearly defined when considering
nursing records. The introduction of the Nursing Process makes it
even more important that nurses decide who controls the information which is contained on assessment and history sheets. In some
places this information is already conveyed to the computer in order
to prepare nursing plans. Within the patient's home the community
sisters have a special responsibility, but in their endeavour to
maintain confidentiality they have to be sure that communications
between the various members of the team do not suffer.

It is possible that the time has come for a group of nurses in each
District to prepare their own Code of Practice to give guidance on
the handling of personal information. This guidance should include
the ethical implications, and be drawn up in association with
medical colleagues and Medical Records Department.

In the future it is likely that the computer will do most of the
written work. However, no mechanical device can take the place of
the spoken word. It has been estimated that 48 per cent of all
communication between one person and another is made up of the
tone of voice and of non-verbal forms of expression. Since the

output of the computer is only as good as the input it receives, if nurses are to use this form of technology they have to learn to give clear, concise and accurate information. Unfortunately many nursing records contain misleading jargon and abbreviations which do not convey anything. To be sure that what is recorded is understood, there has to be a sorting out of much of the language which nurses use. This is urgent and must be recognised as a special skill to be learnt and practised. It also has to be remembered that statistics are not always as helpful as they seem. They are like lamp-posts, they should be used for illumination rather than for leaning upon.

What has been called the 'explosion of information' necessitates discrimination in deciding how much people need to know. Careful scrutiny will often show that much which is communicated is unnecessary, and is not assimilated by those for whom it is intended. The essentials have to be conveyed without omitting the detail which can be of vital importance. In feeding the computer with the nursing plan, the fact that the patient sleeps with only one pillow may be as important as the medication.

6 Teaching and learning

There are several projects established in the United States of America and in Canada which enable nursing students to practise solving nursing problems by means of simulated computer units. Material is collected from actual situations centred around the care of the patient. The object is to help learners to make decisions from a range of alternatives, without the guidance of the teacher.

One of the advantages of computer simulation is that students can learn at their own pace. In addition, nurses in small isolated hospitals can be introduced to situations which they might otherwise never experience, because of the distances which they would have to travel. The only danger would appear to be that nursing decisions could be made in relation to the symptoms of disease, without the human reactions which are so vital. This is one way in which technology can be applied to learning, and the effectiveness has still to be evaluated. It is gaining interest, and has potential both for the qualified nurse and those in the initial stages of their education; however, it must always be remembered that this method is a teaching aid, and can never be a substitute for the personal influence and guidance of the nurse teacher.

Video-tape is being used both in hospital and the community, but needs to be in skilled hands. Whatever value this may have in helping to make learning more realistic, it must not be forgotten that it encroaches on the privacy of the individual. Permission must be obtained in the first instance, and careful explanation is essential about the use of video-tape. Patients should have the opportunity to withhold permission if they wish.

Wisely applied technology has much to offer, and there are centres, such as the Learning Resources Unit at the City Polytechnic, Sheffield, where a whole range of facilities are available to Nurse Teachers. There are also more simple ways in which tape-recordings and slides can be used to reinforce learning for patients. Often they are flustered, and still recovering from their illness, and to be able to sit quietly and hear again what they have been taught can be most helpful. This kind of teaching aid could be very appropriate for the newly diagnosed diabetic patient, but as with nurses learning through computers, this aid must never take the place of personal contact. It is only when the nurse is in close touch with the patient that she can understand the anxieties and unspoken fears which he or she may be trying to express.

The nurse's influence and responsibilities

This very brief survey of technology applied to nursing practice demonstrates some of the attributes which nurses require in order to influence decisions which have to be made. Sometimes it is thought that this is a subject primarily for the medical and administrative staff, and not within the province of nurses, but the examples which have been given show that this is not the case. Nurses must be ready to give their views on research findings, to examine new equipment and weigh up the advantages and disadvantages of its use, keeping the patient's welfare in the forefront. To do this effectively, critical faculties have to be developed, and nurses must not be afraid to ask questions, to search for alternatives, make comparisons, and insist on having the information they require. This analytical approach is vital in an age in which technology must be accepted as part of life.

Since one kind of technology usually invites another, nurses have also to be on the alert for signs of stress among their colleagues as larger buildings are required to house specialised equipment and technical departments. As distances become greater, staff are separated from their companions and feel the loss of their support. There is a special responsibility for the Occupational Health Nurse to watch for such problems.

Finally, nurses have to learn not to be afraid of technology but to welcome what it has to offer. If they are sure of their role and objectives, it is possible to keep a balance between supplying the social and psychological needs of patients and the employment of technical aids towards their care. Allowing the emphasis to fall more heavily in one direction may not only be detrimental to patients, but could destroy the true function of the nurse.

References

1   *Report of House of Commons Social Services Committee on Perinatal and Neonatal Mortality*, Vol. 1. 1980. London: HMSO House of Commons Paper 663–1.
2   Dingwall, R. 1979. Are you ready for the microchip? *Nursing Times*, 7 June.
3   DHSS Circular HC(77) 22 and accompanying letter from the CNO(77) 9.
4   *Report of the Committee on Data Protection*. 1978. London: HMSO, Cmnd 7341.

8

An Environment for Change

'It is so easy to convince ourselves that we are pulling our weight in the world if we perform adequately in our niche, which can also be our very comfortable rut.'

These words were part of a lecture given by Virginia Henderson, research associate emeritus of Yale University.[1] She was speaking of the need for the nurse of the future to feel personally responsible for changing conditions locally, nationally and internationally. It is, however, difficult for an individual nurse to do this if there is no encouragement to use initiative. Sometimes nurses believe that their suggestions will be frowned upon by their superiors, or.that they will be labelled as troublemakers. This is often an attitude of mind passed down from one generation to another, and has no factual basis. On the other hand, the first essential in creating an environment where new ideas can flourish, is that every nurse accepts that a questioning approach to the work done is a professional obligation which cannot be evaded. It is right that professional people should discuss their work in a positive and constructive manner, since only in this way will the changes which are suggested be seen as a contribution toward improvements in nursing care, and not to imply personal criticism.

There seems to be a misconception within the National Health Service that if changes are made in the structure of an organisation, this will solve the problems, but something much more fundamental has to happen. There has to be a willing co-operation and commitment from those within the organisation, firstly to accept that problems exist, and then to be prepared to do something about them. Only in this way will change be effective. What is required is a quality of leadership which encourages people to look critically and purposefully at their work, as well as at the environment in which it is performed. In every group, however small, leaders will emerge, and often some of the most valuable innovations come from the one or two thinking people who have taken the trouble to consider what they are doing and ask questions.

It is worth recalling why innovation and change are necessary. There are four areas where action is required:

1   To solve a problem
2   To apply a principle
3   To introduce a new idea
4   To make an improvement in an existing situation

In spite of the need for progressive thinking, if a proposal does
none of these things it is suspect. It is well to remember that not all
change is for the better. Discrimination and careful weighing up of
the facts are important, so that what is of value is not lost in the
process of change. It may be that if things are going well, it is better
to leave them as they are, but it is essential to be sure all *is* well.

This chapter will not dwell on the major issues, but will give
practical suggestions which can help all nurses, at whatever level in
the hierarchy, to create an environment where change is seen as a
challenge and not as a threat. It can take many months, or even
years, before such an atmosphre becomes a reality. Much depends
on the leaders, and their belief in the ability of the team to influence
standards of nursing care.

An atmosphere of trust

There must be an element of stability in a world where changes are
taking place at a pace never known before. In learning to live with
uncertainty, a search is made for security and for values which are
meaningful. If these cannot be found, people become despondent
and may resist all new ideas in an effort to hold on to what is known
and tried.

The following example shows how an effort was made to supply
this element of security. When preparing a group of some five
hundred nurses to move from a nineteenth century building to a
modern teaching hospital, the first step taken was to make a list of
the policies and methods of working which would not change,
despite the very different environment. There was some adaptation
to be done, but the fundamental principles were to be the same. A
short recording was then made emphasising these facts, and it was
played to each group of nurses on the first session of their orientation
period. This took away much of the fear and apprehension and
contributed to the effectiveness with which they received a large
number of changes over a short period of time.

Perhaps the greatest necessity in building the right environment is
that the nursing team should trust their leader. If they are supported
during their everyday duties, they can usually count on continued

support in time of stress or difficulty. It is essential that there is also a pattern of communication within the group which really works. The channels must go up as well as down and across, and must not be blocked by the presence of an hierarchy. It has been said that 'A bad decision can be rescued by sympathetic handling, and a good one can be ruined by misunderstanding.'[2] Mistakes will sometimes be made, but where there is mutual trust, there is less likelihood that there will be misunderstandings. It is also important to have a sympathetic person with whom to discuss the frustrations and failures, as well as the successes.

Sometimes, when a change is anticipated, the comment is made that the staff organisations will not agree. This is then made an excuse for not pursuing the project. It is implied that there is lack of trust between the leaders and those involved in the situation, and so the idea of a change of any kind is automatically regarded with suspicion. Fear and suspicion can form one of the greatest barriers to effective communication and unless they are removed there will inevitably be a breakdown in relationships. Most industrial troubles occur because of failures in communication at an early stage in the proceedings, thus producing a 'them and us' situation which becomes disruptive, and finally destructive.

There are three important factors in considering Fig. 8.1. Firstly, difficulties grow in intensity when there is a lapse of time before anyone is available to listen to the problem. Secondly, the person who is listening must understand the root cause. This may not be apparent initially, but a perceptive and understanding listener is required who will be sufficiently sensitive to identify the essence of the problem. Thirdly, those who will be affected by change must know who makes decisions, and to whom they can go when they want to discuss anxieties. Sometimes there may be no foundation for such anxiety, which may be based on rumour. Every organisation is affected by the grapevine, and it can be very destructive. It has little use except for spreading good news. However, even if there is no cause for worry, it is important that someone is prepared to give their time to explain the true facts.

Understanding reaction to change

Different personalities, varied experience and a diversity of background, all affect people's attitudes. It is not surprising therefore that an alteration to the pattern of daily life produces a reaction. This can take place in various ways. Sometimes there will be a persistent

EFFECTIVE COMMUNICATION

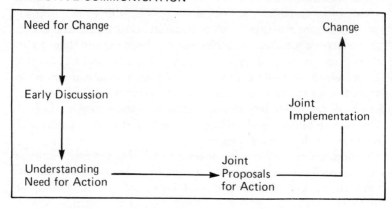

COMMUNICATION OBSTRUCTED

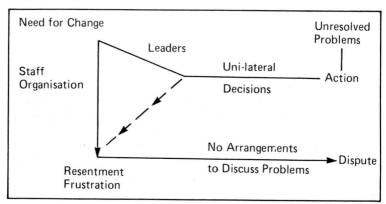

Fig 8.1   Involvement of staff organisations at a time of change

resistance to change, and this rigid approach is very hard to influence. Occasionally, there is a group who do show enthusiasm, but this is short-lived, and soon they give up and want to return to their usual pattern. Another group will persist with a new venture, and really try hard to fulfil the demands made upon them, but perhaps through lack of encouragement or because there are insufficient resources, the members are unable to sustain their efforts, and they find the strain too much. Such circumstances can result in resignations or an increase in sick certificates.

Fortunately, there are people who welcome change, and it is this group who will often volunteer to experiment. If they are successful, it is then easier to expand the project. However, it is still important to remember that within every new proposal there must be an element of continuity to form the foundation. It is when the whole system is discarded that problems arise, for there is nothing familiar left for those who are affected.

It is an understandable human reaction that people affected by change think first about what it will do to them personally. There may be a genuine fear of losing status if additional qualifications and knowledge are insisted upon in order to do tasks which in the past, have been done by achieving solely practical skills. Experience is thus seen to be subordinated to earning a certificate. This can be a very real problem in an age of computers and technology. There may be fear of redundancy if scope for promotion is seen to be reduced. Assurances that the person concerned will not lose financially will not heal the hurt. The most sensitive area upon which the innovator can tread is that of the accumulated experience of the more senior members of the group, for it appears that the personal worth of these members is being brought into question. In such circumstances it is easy to understand that it may be easier to oppose change than to admit an inability to cope.

Reference has already been made (see p. 59) to the necessity to find the root cause of a problem. Excuses for avoiding a new proposal, such as lack of staff, money, or time, or even comments such as 'the doctors won't like it', may mask anxiety or lack of interest. Sometimes the claim that there is insufficient time is due to the reluctance of nurses to relinquish tasks which have become part of the routine. The making of beds was questioned in a ward for elderly patients, and it was found that these were made again each morning following treatments, even though the night staff had performed this task only a few hours previously.

New ideas may be obstructed because of preoccupation with the organisational aspects, and even the underlying objective can become obscured. For example, when a group of nurses were revising the nursing records as a means of improving communication between those caring for the patient, discussion was hampered by the constant reference to where the records should be stored. It is the task of the leader to try to remove such obstacles and as many problems as possible should be anticipated so that solutions can be found in advance.

It is often said that attitudes cannot be changed, but this is not so. People can be greatly influenced by their environment, by colleagues, and by their leaders, if they respect them and appreciate what they are trying to accomplish.

Encouraging a creative spirit

An environment where there is freedom to question and scrutinise is
a healthy one. It means that people know what actually takes place,
and not what they think happens. This has been well described by
Professor J. Hayward.[3] His research showed that many nurses are
skilled in using small talk and social chat in the belief that they are
reassuring the patient, but in fact this may be of more benefit to the
nurse. It has not been properly considered in this instance, what
'reassurance' really is. If this questioning approach is to flourish there
must be security among the nursing team. They have to accept that
the way they have performed in the past may not be the best and so
be willing to try alternative methods. For this they need support and
encouragement, and the opportunity to use initiative. To be creative
there has to be freedom to make choices. This is apparent when
skilled nurses play with children. They are inventive and use the
opportunities presented by the children to try out new games, so
that each moment is enjoyed to the full. In so doing the nurses find
pleasure and fulfilment. It is not necessary to attempt large projects
in order to be creative, but there must be the freedom to use
experience and personal gifts. Without such opportunity there will
be frustration and apathy.

However, nurses should also understand the limits of this
freedom. For example, there are occasions when the lack of specific
training or experience must restrict activity so that no harm is caused
to others. The amount of scope which leaders will allow the team
depends very much on their own feelings of security; they have to
be able to welcome the success of others. There is a useful prayer
which emphasises this; 'Lord make me humble enough to accept the
advice of others, and to let them do what I think I can do better
myself.' The embodies a true understanding of what status is all
about. It is a strength brought about by influence, which enables
both the leader and the team to grow together, each influencing the
other. Within this situation there is room for maximising the
strengths, rather than concentrating on the weaknesses. If enthusiasm is nurtured there can be some pleasant surprises and
rewarding experiences.

Maintaining the environment and planning ahead

To sustain an atmosphere conducive to change there must be regular
testing of the effectiveness of the communication network to detect

weaknesses and correct them. A review of policies and objectives must also be done to ensure that these remain relevant.

Sometimes a change will come unexpectedly, but usually there is some indication that it is pending. It is unwise to ignore such warnings in the hope that ultimately the change will not take place. Preparation can be made in case it happens, and indeed with skilled planning some innovations can be made unobtrusively over the course of time.

In order to prepare for impending change, it is helpful if the leader extends the existing skills of the individual members of the team. This places emphasis on their personal performance, rather than the title of the job, or place in the hierarchy. It makes the boundaries of the job more flexible, and encourages members to share their expertise. There may be retraining to be done and this can be undertaken in advance. To ask people to assume new responsibilities for which they have not had the necessary preparation is unfair and unjustified.

The following example shows how important it is to keep looking ahead even if it may seem impossible to implement a course of action at the time it is suggested. A small group of community nurses prepared a project which showed how the care of the patients in one of the hospital wards for the elderly could be improved by joint staffing between the community and hospital nurses. Unfortunately the ward in question would not easily adapt to the suggestion without structural alteration. The project was well received but there was no money available to implement it. However, as a first step the proposals were discussed and the plans for the new lay-out of the ward were considered by the experts and costed. Meanwhile the opportunity was taken to send some of the nurses to visit a hospital where this kind of teamwork was working successfully. Twelve months passed, and then a telephone call was received from the Regional Health Authority, saying that they wished to spend a sum of money on the hospital to make improvements in the care of the elderly patients. All that was needed was to take the nursing project out of the file and give it to the Administrator.

Controlling the outcome

The control of any project begins when the objectives are determined. It is at this stage that the means of evaluation should be decided. Those who have been taking part need to know if they

have been successful, so that they receive the praise which is their
due. Even if total success has not been achieved, it is still important to
share the knowledge which has been gained. It may prevent the
same mistakes being made again, and such experiences are opportunities for growth and progress. Information should be written
down and not just committed to memory. Nurses have yet to
acquire the habit of putting facts and figures on paper which may be
of value not only at that particular time, but in the future.

Nurses who investigate change may choose to delegate the
evaluation of the project to those who take part. An objective
assessment is essential to make sure that the results are seen to be fair
and without bias. Entrusting this important task to the group
themselves provides additional stimulus. Leaders who delegate in
this way need not fear loss of influence or control, since the more
sharing that takes place, the greater will be the willingness to achieve
mutual goals. Within this kind of environment struggles for
authority do not arise, since the purpose of the undertaking is
paramount. This provides the motivation necessary for success, and
control is achieved not by any one person, but by the combined
endeavour of all who are participating.

References

1   Henderson, V. 1980. Nursing yesterday and tomorrow. *Nursing
    Times*, 22 May. (First of an annual series of lectures at Royal
    Marsden Hospital.)
2   Beardwell, M. and Dearden, B. 1979. Management style as a
    key component of industrial relations policy. *Health Services
    Manpower Review*, November (Vol. 5, No. 4).
3   Hayward, J. 1975. 'Information — a prescription against pain.'
    London, Rcn.

PART II

The Scope of Nursing

9
The Nurse's Response to Society

Interaction and involvement

'You see, I am a nurse.' This short phrase is often the explanation given for the particular way in which help has been given to a member of the public. It implies that nurses have qualities and expertise which enable them to make a special contribution. Society expects this contribution to be of a particular standard, and more will be said about this in a later chapter. But what is meant by society? The Universal English dictionary describes it as 'a fellowship, community or association which exists for mutual protection and help.' Perhaps this concept of society as an institution for giving rather than receiving is one that has not had sufficient emphasis. However, this definition clarifies the relationship between nurse and patient which is the main theme of this book. It is a kind of partnership in the provision of care, rather than an unquestioning acceptance of what is offered. Mutual protection and help mean safe care and also shared care.

Since nurses are part of society and not outside it, they participate in the formation of attitudes, values and the culture within society. They bring to the profession the products of the environment in which they live and work. It is therefore important that nurses recognise the sociological factors which have an impact on their work and on their activities as citizens. In developing this social awareness, they are more likely to be usefully involved in the life of the community. Fig. 9.1 illustrates the many social factors which influence the different age groups, and how the sum of these can shape the pattern of society.

In the first instance, it will be helpful to study those aspects of society which are of particular significance to the objectives of the health services, and which can influence decisions about nursing care (see Fig. 9.2). They can be listed as follows:

a) Home, family and work
b) Language as a means of communication
c) Culture and custom
d) Education and values
e) Public affairs

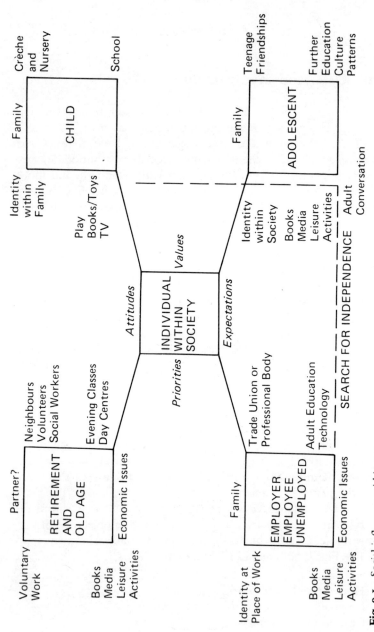

Fig 9.1 Social influences within age groups

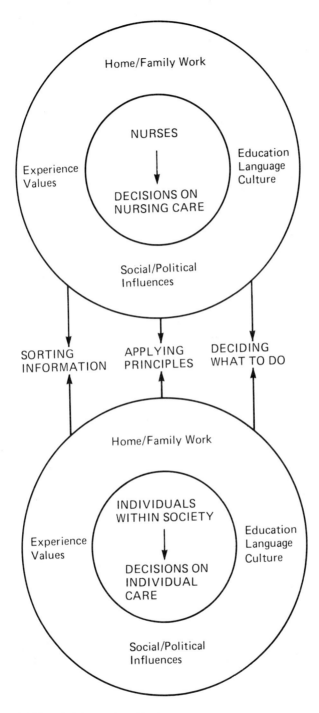

Fig 9.2 Making decisions – the wider issues

a)   Home, family and work

Most people have experienced at some time the discomfort of being
within a depressing environment, one which lacks the familiar
things which are essential to their well-being. The word 'familiar'
comes from the same root as 'family' and speaks of things which
make us feel at home. Perhaps it is right that in considering the
different environments from which patients come for help, first
thoughts should be about those who have no fixed abode. In some
parts of the country organisations have been set up for their care, and
at least one city has appointed a nurse to hold clinics to deal with
minor problems and make referrals to the general practitioner. She
works closely with the Salvation Army, the police and the local
voluntary organisations. It is a reflection on society that such
arrangements are necessary, but with rising unemployment the
situation could get worse.

Many of these 'patients' are familiar to the sisters or charge nurses
in charge of Accident Departments, but in changing the name and
nature of these departments, it may be that the Health Service has
excluded these 'casual' visitors and left them without the help they
need. This is not a problem which nurses can solve on their own, but
it requires the combined effort and determination of the professionals in the health and social services and the help of members of
the community as well.

It has been said that poverty is as pathogenic as microbes. It would
seem logical, therefore, that nurses are as concerned about poor
housing as they are about the control of infection. Perhaps it would
be better to accelerate the housing programmes and prevent some of
the repeated admissions to hospital which are the result of such
living conditions. Doctors and nurses are becoming more aware of
these matters, but in their efforts to meet the increasing demands
made upon them and to reduce long waiting-lists, there is a
tendency to overlook the situation which created the illness in the
first place. It is a tragedy that a sense of urgency is often lacking when
help is required in a situation of serious poverty. The death of a 14
month-old boy, starved and frozen to death, only two months after
a report had been made on his social circumstances, is an indictment
on those responsible.[1] It seems that the lessons are never learnt, and
that in an effort to provide teamwork, there is a reluctance for
anyone to make decisions. Conferences and meetings have their
place, but someone has to ensure that a plan of action is not only
agreed, but implemented.

In December 1979 a report was published entitled *Poverty in the*

United Kingdom.[2] The author states that poverty is relative to the living standards existing at the time. This is a point to remember when discussing the plan of nursing care so that impractical suggestions are not made. Nurses are aware of the economic restraints on the health services, but they may not always be quick to realise situations where there are real financial difficulties among their patients. With the help of the social worker, relief can be obtained, but it requires tact and sensitivity, and knowledge of the voluntary agencies which can provide assistance.

Any thoughts about the family cover such a wide spectrum that only a few aspects can be mentioned. The increasing number of elderly members of society must be of concern to nurses. It was said earlier that nurses share the values and attitudes of society. It is essential, therefore, that every nurse questions her own approach to an ageing population. Sadly, all too often the presence of elderly patients is considered a problem. There is a tendency to request transfer for such patients to the geriatric ward or old people's home, and perpetuate the attitude of a society which relinquishes the responsibility to someone else. Nurses must influence this attitude by their belief in the personal worth of the individual – which includes the elderly. Everyone needs to be valued or there is no meaning to life.

> The need to care about others and to be cared about, to feel and give affection and love, is fundamental and universal. There is no evidence that people ever lose the need for warmth and affection in their lives.[3]

Bertrand Russell said that 'Civilization is concerned with values independent of utility.' Unfortunately, modern society emphasises productivity and quantity rather than quality. Yet there is much to be learnt from those with a life-time of experience, and society is incomplete without old people who create the 'wholeness' of family life. Instead of spending time and money in finding places for the elderly in purpose built accommodation, it might be better to concentrate on how they can be given their rightful place *within* society.

A large part of human life is spent working – that is if the person is fortunate enough to have employment. Nurses are seldom without a job and the work they do is stimulating and rewarding. It may be difficult for them to imagine the stigma of being jobless, or how demoralising it can be to work on a conveyor belt doing a monotonous task. The kind of job you do makes you behave in a certain way. It is like people acting in a play, they assume a particular role. Certain jobs have status in the eyes of society, and this can influence how the job is approached, and whether or not it is seen to be worthwhile. Status is linked with the increasing demand for 'paper' qualifications and the pressure to seek promotion. The lack of employment in a technological age and in a society with many economic restraints is disturbing.

There is a danger that unless the nurse can try to understand more about other people's jobs, vital clues will be missed when deciding on the nursing plan. For example, an elderly man was admitted to hospital and was given a sedative to help him to sleep during his first night in the ward. At about midnight, he became disorientated and obstreperous. He was given further sedation. The next morning one of the nurses sat down and talked to him. She learnt that he was a night watchman, and that he had not been to bed at night for many years. When he awoke, he thought that the nurse was an intruder on his premises and so he took action. This is an illustration where time spent in the first instance could have avoided much distress.

In order to have a better understanding of the local industry, nurses can take the initiative and see for themselves — even if it means going down a mine. The Occupational Health Nurse of a large factory is a well-informed colleague who can give much help and advice. The nurses who have spent most of their careers in a rural district may have little idea of the attitudes and problems which are prevalent in an industrial city. However, without this knowledge, they may have difficulty in understanding what the patient is trying to explain.

So far, rehabilitation has not featured very much in the life of the predominantly hospital trained nurse. Finding work when you are handicapped is hard enough, but it is even more difficult when the labour market is highly competitive. It can be most revealing to learn of the trauma experienced by those who have recently lost their sight through accident or illness. Making a cup of tea is a major exercise if you cannot see, and skills such as potato peeling have to be painstakingly learnt so that fingers are not damaged in the process. Nurses need to be aware of the many aids to living which can help the handicapped to become independent, and a period in the rehabilitation workshop can help them to learn by actually doing the job alongside the trainee.

In some of the large General Hospitals, the Disabled Resettlement Officer has a permanent office, and the importance of his task as a member of the rehabilitation team is well recognised. Nurses need to get to know something of the work of this Officer so that they can take their part in giving the physically and the mentally handicapped the support and understanding they require, as they seek to establish themselves again in society.

b) *Language as a means of communication*

If the word 'society' is meant to convey a fellowship of people living together as a community, language must be a vital tool in providing the means for mutual understanding. Language can link people together, but only if the words which are used convey successfully the speaker's meaning. It is not always realised that there are many people with a restricted vocabulary, who have difficulty in interpreting unfamiliar words. Sometimes nurses forget this, and they not only use technical jargon, but also words which have frightening connotations. 'Pneumonia' is one that to some people means a disease which kills, since the difference in prognosis with the advent of antibiotics is not appreciated.

Dialects in different parts of the country can also inhibit understanding, and may produce as many problems as a foreign language. A meaningful framework for dialogue can only be acquired by association with the people concerned, and the will to try to appreciate what they wish to convey.

People communicate not only through utterance, but also behaviour. Gestures and body language can express all kinds of messages to the observant listener. It is revealing to watch a deaf person tell a story using the British sign language. This is a most descriptive means of communication which can be of inestimable value to those who not only cannot hear, but have associated speech problems.

Body language can be a more reliable indication of how a person is feeling than the words they use. Marian Chace, a psychiatric nurse in the United States of America who was the pioneer of dance therapy, believed that

> the gestures and habits which we bring with us from infancy are as significant to those who deal closely with us as the words we choose to communicate our distress or our happiness. To interpret this movement language is the primary task of the dance therapist. [4]

There are other factors which have an effect on language, such as intelligence, memory and experience. Lack of access to the written word can severely hamper the ability to communicate. Those who have recently become visually handicapped will often have lost the art of spelling correctly, and may have to learn new skills to overcome this. They can be helped by a simple introduction to the use of phonetics and spelling rules.

For those who have not acquired the basic skills of reading and writing during their general education — often through no fault of their own — much is being done by the 'On the Move' literacy movement. Volunteer teachers will visit a client at home or participate in sessions at the local Adult Education College.

In trying to understand those who come to this country from overseas, it is sometimes helpful to try to imagine the transition which the newcomer has to undergo, for example, someone from an Asian village who is to live in a town in Britain:

Shopping. At home, everyday needs would usually be obtained from the fields or the local bazaars. The supermarket is unknown. Consider the bewilderment of seeing the mass of produce on the shelves all labelled and priced!

Transport. Flocks of animals are more likely to be passing through the village street than motorised transport. Imagine the terrifying impact of the traffic, and attempting to understand how to use the pedestrian crossings.

Medical services. If these have existed at all in the village, they may have been limited to the occasional visit of the medical auxiliary or the missionary nurse. Maternal and perinatal deaths will not be uncommon. Contrast this with what is offered to those who attend an ante-natal clinic at a health centre in this country.

It is unlikely that the media will have had much effect on preparing the Asian visitor for life in Britain, but for many this will have greatly influenced their impressions, and therefore their attitudes. Programmes on radio and television can usefully inform, but they can also give fragmented and incomplete information which is disturbing to the listener. This can be particularly so in relation to programmes about health and disease. This fact needs to be remembered when nurses are trying to find out what patients already know about their particular health problems. Members of the caring professions must be ready to take part in programmes on the media and provide accurate and helpful information for the public, in a language they can readily understand. In this way they can influence attitudes towards health in a positive and constructive manner. Such participation also promotes good relationships between the professions and those who control this important method of communication, and they will often give their help in return. For example, a group of nurses in a large city were so upset by the trauma which they saw in the children's ward where they worked, that with the help of local radio they made an appeal to parents to pay more regard to the safety of children on the roads.

c) Culture and custom

Thoughts about language must lead to consideration of the social skills which are an essential part of communication. To establish mutual respect and understanding requires humility, and the willingness to see things from another point of view.

Social skills are part of the culture of any society, and these are passed on from one generation to another. Culture is not the same as custom, which is akin to habit. The customs of a particular society are the product of the feelings, beliefs and attitudes which are held to be of value, and which are essential to everyday living.

Although it may be thought by the doctors, nurses and architects that mixed sex wards are preferable, not every patient will find this acceptable, and allowance must be made for alternative accommodation. For some, there are dietary habits which are essential to religious observance. Acknowledging this fact, a catering manager in an area where there are many people of West Indian origin, holds Open Days so that they can come and talk with the kitchen staff. In this way the cooks learn at first hand the needs of their potential patients.

d) Education and values

Many nurses will be members of parent/teacher associations, and may be the first to know about changes in the educational system. An instance of such a change is the Warnock Report[5] which recommends the inclusion of handicapped children in the ordinary schools. Knowledge of the special developmental needs of these children is essential in order to advise teachers, and parents can draw attention to the expertise available from school nurses already working in this field.

The links between the general educational system and nursing education will be discussed later, but the nurse's response to society must include acknowledgement of the values which are instilled during school life and in the home. These eventually become the accepted patterns of behaviour, signifying what is desirable and therefore worth pursuing by the community as a whole. However, when considering the application of the nursing ethic in Chapter 6, it was found that nurses will not always be able to accept society's estimation of what is right or wrong, since this can conflict with professional thinking.

It has been said that the community obtains the kind of society it wants, and the members shape their own destiny. If this is true, it is difficult to understand the increasing amount of violence which is so evident. No longer can the management of the aggressive patient be confined to those with a knowledge of psychiatry. All nurses need this knowledge, so that they can recognise circumstances which may precipitate a violent reaction and prevent its occurrence. The problems are often social ones, and are partly due to the abandonment of a firm foundation on which a code of behaviour was previously based.

This loss of a firm foundation on which to establish a way of life may also be responsible for the increase in problems such as alcoholism and drug addiction. There are seven thousand known alcoholics in the country and the number is on the increase. Since this situation has been largely created by sociological factors, it is reasonable that individual members should assume some responsibility for the resulting problems. Nurses, however, sometimes question this and suggest that to interfere is an infringement of the rights of the individual to order his life as he wishes. It is true that individual rights must be respected, but the nurse has certain obligations which cannot be avoided. The International Code of Nursing Ethics states that 'the nurse conserves life, alleviates suffering *and* promotes health.' Those responsible for nursing education are therefore making certain that information about problem drinking is given to nurses so that they can recognise it where it exists and also take part in the prevention of alcohol misuse and the promotion of health education. The Joint Board of Clinical Nursing Studies has a special course of preparation for those nurses undertaking care of alcoholics as members of multidisciplinary teams.

In facing social problems such as alcoholism and drug addiction, nurses must be absolutely sure that they are aware of the implications. They can then explain them clearly and confidently to the patient, to ensure the significance of what is happening is fully understood. The physical complications, the risks to health, and the implications if the facilities of the health service are not available at the crucial moment, must be clearly identified. Such explanation has to be given with sensitivity and without implying criticisms so that there is mutual trust. The advice is then more likely to be acceptable.

e)   Public affairs

There is an understandable reluctance among nurses to enter the political arena, and many consider that politics and professionalism do not mix. Baroness McFarlane, the first nurse to enter the House of Lords, expressed her concern on entering the political scene, and emphasised the importance of seeing that the right decisions prevailed. [6] She also stressed that if nurses do not involve themselves in the making of decisions about health care, they have no right to criticise the outcome. It is not easy to separate nursing from the views held by society and the politicians, and ultimately it is the government of the day who decide the policy and the direction that the health services will take. It is when the political view-point overrides what is right and necessary that members of society are needed who will speak in support of those who may be unable to do so for themselves. This is of special importance in relation to local government affairs. By getting to know their local councillors, nurses can not only put forward positive ideas, but also prevent problems which affect the daily lives of those in the community. It is often the nurse who knows from practical experience how difficult it is to obtain a prescription from the chemist if the 'bus services are curtailed.

Nurses have a particular contribution to make when decisions are made about the environment. Perhaps if nurses had been more vocal, the architects and planners would have had second thoughts about high-rise flats, and the building of housing estates at a distance from the shops and public transport. Nurses working within the community have a very real understanding of the loneliness which such developments can create, not only for the elderly, but for young mothers.

Working with volunteers

Several examples have been given of ways in which nurses respond to the needs of society. However, they do not do this alone, and increasingly volunteer groups such as the Samaritans, Cruse, and the Good Neighbour Schemes, are giving help in times of crisis. Nurses have sometimes regarded the voluntary helper as the 'filler in' of gaps for which professional workers cannot provide. There is a need for a change of attitude which accepts volunteers as people working in their own right, who are respected for their specific contribution. This is essential if they are to feel welcome and find satisfaction on the job.

It is questionable whether it is right, or even possible, to rely on the health services to meet all the demands. If there is to be a return to caring *within* the community, it should be possible for those with professional knowledge to share this, and give support to the volunteers in the background. The following episode illustrates this point. A group of volunteers were organising an outing for those who were deaf and had a visual handicap. It was decided that they would take them to the sea, and to the local museum. However, on hearing about this, someone with special knowledge of these handicaps, tactfully suggested that the first step might be to ask the group themselves for their ideas. The request was for a visit to the local park to feel and smell the flowers, to touch the grass and explore the natural textures of the environment. Volunteer and professional must learn to work alongside, as partners, each giving a contribution of equal importance.

Contributing and responding to the life of the community can be most satisfying. It is also possible that an interest in a particular sphere of activity is stimulated whilst the nurse is working, which on retirement can fulfil the continued desire to be needed and provide a service.

References

1   Allen-Mills, T. 1981. Report on Malcolm Page. *Daily Telegraph*, 28 March.
2   Townsend, P. 1979. *Poverty in the United Kingdom – A Survey of Household Resources and Standards of Living*. Harmondsworth: Penguin.
3   *Improving Geriatric Care in Hospital*. 1975. British Geriatrics Society and Rcn.
4   Puttock, D. 1981. Within our reach – a report on dance therapy for psychiatric patients. *Nursing Times*, 26 March.
5   *Report of the Committee of Inquiry into the Education of Handicapped*

Children and Young People (Warnock Report). 1978. London: HMSO, Cmnd 7212.
6 Nurses in the political arena. Report on annual conference of the Nursing Studies Association of the University of Edinburgh, May 1980. 1980. *Nursing Times*, 29 May.

The Nurse's Influence at Work

A glance at Fig. 10.1 below gives some indication of the many places in which nurses give their services.

Figure 10.2 illustrates the diverse circumstances in which nurses meet people. This suggests that they should work toward a deeper understanding of human behaviour and relationships as an important part of their extended role. This becomes even more apparent when looking at the many different people with whom nurses collaborate and communicate. It is important to remember that this is done throughout a twenty four hour period; many of the contacts, therefore, are made in circumstances not experienced by the working population as a whole.

Fig 10.1 The nurse's influence at work

Fig 10.2 Nursing contacts

The nurse's contribution and influence

The purpose of this chapter is to consider what nurses have to offer to those of other disciplines with whom they work — the contribution which goes beyond the actual giving of care to patients and produces good teamwork. This does not necessarily relate to the position a particular nurse holds in the organisation, but is dependent on applying professional knowledge and experience to the problems which occur where the work is done.

The amount of influence which is generated depends largely on the extent to which nurses earn respect among their colleagues, and on what they have to offer. There are some contributions which nurses make in the course of their work which are not yet

sufficiently recognised. It is these which will now be given attention
since they will have increasing significance in the health service of
the future.

The nurse as educator

We will not concentrate at this point on the qualified nurse teachers.
Their influence in the School or College of Nursing is inherent in
their special rôle. In larger educational establishments such as the
Universities, they are a minority group and yet are having a
considerable impact on the life and work of the institution as their
influence grows. However, the majority of nurse teachers work
alongside their colleagues in the nursing service. This vital partnership will be discussed in Part III.

Professor R. S. Peters said,[1]

'Education consists in initiating others into activities, modes of
conduct and thought which have standards written into them, by
reference to which, it is possible to act, think and feel, with
varying degrees of skill.'

Two words in this quotation are particularly illuminating: firstly the
word 'initiating'. The difference between education and training lies
in the fact that to educate is to introduce new concepts and avenues
of thought which enable others to have an enhanced or different
understanding from that which they previously possessed. The
educator thus enables the learners to seek further knowledge for
themselves, and inspires them to do so. Training, on the other hand,
is limited to the acquisition of a sequence of specific skills, often
involving the use of equipment. Once the procedure is understood,
a satisfactory level of performance is obtained by practice and
repetition. The trainer tells the learner what to do, but not
necessarily why it is done.

The second word which Professor Peters uses which is particularly significant is 'standards'. He implies that the educator knows
the goal toward which the learner is being directed. To be able to
identify learning objectives is one of the most important tasks to be
undertaken by the qualified nurse, and an essential one if the place of
work is recognised by the General Nursing Council for the purposes
of nurse education. It is a difficult assignment, but an excellent
mental exercise. Good examples are to be found in the publications
concerning the courses of the Joint Board of Clinical Nursing
Studies. Meaningful objectives include the skills to be learnt, the

relevant knowledge to accompany them, and the attitudes which are inherent in the final achievement. Further thought to the preparation of nurses and their continuing education will be given in Chapter 15. However it is important to remember that *every* nurse can find opportunities for educating, if she or he is prepared to find the reasons why certain rules and procedures are adopted, and the implications of the contribution made by other members of the team.

An example can be given regarding the domestic staff who play such an important part in maintaining the service. They follow a ward routine, faithfully performing tasks according to a work list; however, these tasks cannot be set in context and have meaning unless the reason for doing them is understood, and it is unlikely that without this knowledge they will always fulfil what is required. It may not be appreciated that it is necessary to discard the duster when leaving the isolation cubicle because a short cut could lead to a spread of infection. Even the knocking of a bedstead may not be appreciated as harmful to the patient, unless it is known that this causes pain. Very few people who have not been patients can fully realise the trauma of noise, and that clattering heels, cups and pails, are very irksome. It was this kind of explanation which was intended to be part of the sapiential authority to which the Salmon Report referred. 'Sapiens', the Latin word meaning 'wise' implies in this context the giving of wisdom acquired by the nurse by virtue of professional knowledge. Perhaps a better phrase would have been 'education for usefulness'. This is not something which can be abandoned and left to the functional manager; the nurse has special knowledge to impart.

The same requirement for the nurse to explain the reason 'why', extends to the ward clerk, who may not always understand the importance of maintaining information about patients in the strictest confidence, and the legal and personal implications of a failure to do so.

An area where there is much scope for the nurse concerns the education of medical students. (See also p. 39.) The future members of the medical profession have a need, and a right, to share in new concepts of nursing care and understand why certain policies and procedures are followed. How else can the medical and nursing partnership which has been described become a reality? Joining the nursing team in the community as well as in the hospital for periods of the day and night under the guidance of the team leader can be a worthwhile experience, as can observing a reporting session or attending a ward meeting.

It can be argued that a great deal of teaching takes place by example as the work progresses. This is true, but in itself it only reinforces current attitudes whereby it is sometimes considered sufficient to understand the application of nursing skill, without thinking much about being a nurse. This has to be explained, for it entails those intangible qualities of compassion, sensitivity and imagination, and also the ability to comprehend how to perform in a particular situation and why it is necessary to do so. The Rev. Michael Wilson summarised this important part of the nurse's role as follows: [2]

> Few professions work continuously so near to the quick of life, its joys and sorrows, suffering, death and human triumphs, and it is those who have faced life as it comes, experienced and reflected upon it, who make educators for humanness.

There is a facet of nursing which can be learnt readily by example, and this concerns attitudes. Trainees in hospital administration have been known to learn much about the tactful handling of a patient's complaint from an experienced ward sister. Where the leaders are courteous and maintain a positive and helpful approach, similar attitudes are adopted by those who are influenced by them, so that ultimately the total environment is affected.

Effective learning is a two-way process. Good teachers are constantly acquiring new knowledge during the process of imparting their own. They are able to do this because they have the will and the humility to accept what others have to give.

Counselling

> Counselling is a way of helping people to help themselves . . . it consists of listening, understanding and accepting; and communicating this understanding to those needing help, so that they are enabled to accept and come to terms with their difficulties, using their own resources. [3]

This definition of counselling suggests the use of skills which all nurses should have developed, for they are the essential equipment for assessing and meeting the needs of patients and clients. The nurse should therefore be well placed to act as a counsellor to anyone seeking help. However, the tendency is still to produce the answers rather than facilitate the outcome, and there is great value in attending one of the courses recognised by the British Association of Counselling, in order to learn more about these skills. The difference between giving advice and true counselling is then fully appreciated.

People who need help will choose the person in whom they feel they can confide. They seek someone who is approachable, and a good listener. Often counsellors are chosen because they have shown that they uphold certain values during the course of their work, and can be trusted. Keeping confidences is so much part of professional life, and yet those standards set without question for patients, may not always be the same for colleagues at work. Nurses can do much to influence this problem where it exists by refusing to take part in indiscreet talk, and tactfully pointing out how damaging it can be.

The effective counsellor is on the alert for the occasion when help is needed. Some years ago, when senior nursing staff in hospital were normally resident, the Matron returned to her flat after finishing her work. She changed into mufti ready to go out. It was then that she remembered she had left a book she wanted on her desk. On the way back to the office, she saw someone leaning against the wall outside, obviously upset. The Matron recognised a member of the staff and offered help. 'Yes please, but you are off-duty,' came the quick response. The Matron invited her into the office and prepared to listen. It was one and a half hours later that she returned to the flat, but a young woman who had been prepared to take her life had changed her mind.

Giving support on the job

Giving support is part of teamwork and it is characteristic of those places where people find security and enjoy their job. The laundry worker who has the nurse's support will not have to spend time extracting soiled linen placed in the wrong bag, or articles of equipment which have been carelessly discarded. If there are difficulties in obtaining supplies of clean linen, a personal visit to the laundry to find out the problems may be more fruitful than a formal complaint. In one hospital the ward sisters took the initiative to invite the laundry sorters to the wards so that they could see the usage for the various items they were handling. This made the work much more meaningful for the laundry staff, and established a relationship with the nurses which helped them both.

Where there is mutual support, a working partnership can develop between disciplines which can greatly benefit the service.

For example, working closely with the Community Physician, nurses in the hospital as well as the community will find they have access to valuable information to help them when planning the service. Perhaps there is something to be learnt from nurses in Kuwait[4] who before establishing the type of nursing service they required, prepared a profile of the community by asking the following questions:

1   Population — age distribution — ratio of men to women — ethnic population?
2   Economic situation — types of industry — amount of employment?
3   Modernisation/urbanisation — housing situation, access to transport shops and amenities?
4   Educational Development — schools, colleges, university provision?
5   Social Characteristics — mobility — special culture patterns.

In view of social trends in this country such information is essential if the type of health care which is really required is to be provided. Knowledge of employment and of the leisure facilities in a district is vital when jobs are few. If in a large city many mothers go to work, nurseries will be needed. Ways of linking this provision with the university have been explored in at least one district as a means of finding mutual assistance through shared accommodation and staffing.

If this kind of detailed picture of the community is prepared, the differences in the needs of urban and rural areas are easier to recognise. The fallacy of having national norms for staffing levels is also apparent when all the relevant factors are assembled.

Completion of questionaires and forms can be a tiresome chore when there is other seemingly more important work to be done. However, it has to be appreciated that the information obtained provides the essential tools for the Community Physician to support nursing colleagues. The statistical graph carefully prepared by a nurse can influence decisions and subsequent policy. In one of the large industrial cities, the nurses in the Accident Department were concerned about the increasing number of attendances by drug addicts. This was causing disruption to the service and pressure on the medical beds. The situation was not given proper attention by the employing authority until the Sister in Charge had prepared meticulous graphs giving not only the attendances, but other helpful nursing information. This was passed on to the Community

Physician who was then able to raise the issue of special treatment facilities in the city.

This kind of working partnership can also be seen where the health visitors in a large group practice are assisting general practitioners by compiling a picture of the social background of the patients who are aged over 75 years. They also perform simple screening as a preventive measure. Their records include the name of a neighbour who can be called in an emergency if there is no relative nearby. In giving this support the health visitors are not taking on medical duties, but by providing a system of routine observations, they are enabling the doctors to give medical supervision where it is most needed, and to pay regular routine visits to those at risk.

Nurses can support their colleagues when financial matters are under consideration. Often a request from one department will indirectly help them, such as the buying of efficient food containers so that the meals for patients are properly heated.

There are occasions when a member of staff in another discipline is meeting opposition in an attempt to uphold standards. It may be the Supplies Officer pressing to retain the quality of drawsheets or a more complex matter involving attitudes and courtesy to patients. In these situations, nurses can give weight to an argument by sharing their intimate knowledge of what is right for patients, and what is professionally acceptable. This kind of support is not given exclusively by nurse managers; those who are close to the patient have first hand knowledge, and should not hesitate to give their views. Sometimes the hierarchy inhibits the nurses' contribution, especially when there are firm lines of demarcation between jobs. If there is to be effective teamwork with all disciplines, the person best equipped to give support must be allowed to do so, regardless of position.

Initiating action

Where people work together in a group, they appreciate a leader who gets things done. They like to feel that their requirements are taken seriously, and that they can be produced with reasonable ease and speed. However, sometimes the actual needs of a particular working group may not be apparent to the members. This may be because they are too close to the situation to recognise them, or they may not have had sufficient opportunity to contrast their perform-ance with others in similar circumstances. Members of other disciplines may have valuable suggestions to make if there is a willingness to accept them. The problems arise when a 'territory' is jealously guarded because it is earmarked as the responsibility of a particular group. Because of their involvement in the continuing care of patients and their families, nurses may be the first people to recognise a deficiency in the service which could be rectified. All too often, however, this becomes a subject for complaint among nurses themselves, and positive action is withheld on the grounds that the matter is the responsibility of another department. This shows a failure in understanding the basis of good teamwork, since the adherence to organisational patterns of responsibility has become more important than the achievement of the corporate objective.

Supposing a nurse is accompanying a relative to the viewing chapel after the death of a member of the family. The nurse will often be the only one to share this very personal service, and therefore has to be especially alert to anything which makes the relative's ordeal harder to bear. For example, any untidyness in the approach to the chapel, and the freshness of plants and flowers need to be noted. Before this journey is taken, a check that all is in order within the chapel is just as much the nurse's responsibility as that of the person in charge of the mortuary. The nurse will be looking for those things which are important to the relative and which may not be apparent to the attendant. If there is room for improvement, a tactful word with the administrator responsible is all that is required.

This corporate effort to maintain standards over the service as a whole works both ways. There has to be no resentment by nurses when justifiable criticism is made to them in the interest of the patient's welfare.

Nurses can instigate action in other ways. Sometimes the frustration of not being able to obtain agreement for the purchase of a seemingly essential item is because too little effort has been made to explain the reason why it is so vital. The importance of having Radio-call to link community nursing sisters with each other and with their patients at night, may only be fully appreciated by taking a member of the management team on an evening visit to a block of high-rise flats. Such an invitation is usually much appreciated.

Sometimes nurses can give great assistance by sharing information which they originally prepared for their own use. Three Health Visitors in an industrial city were aware of the importance of having readily available the details about the various organisations to which they referred. Sometimes it was necessary, for example, to know all the agencies who provide help for the client with a colostomy, or following mastectomy. They decided to make a comprehensive alphabetical file for reference which they called the

'Convenient Relevant Information Bank' or CRIB. This was publicised throughout the city for the use of all community and hospital staff of any discipline, social workers, teachers, or anyone who needed this help. It is kept up to date by a small team of health visitors, and it is intended to have copies made so that these are available at strategic points throughout the city. It has been so useful that other employing authorities are interested in setting up a similar store of information.

Representing a staff organisation

The word 'represent' may be defined as 'to cause to be understood', and nurses have a responsibility to interpret their function and objectives to those with whom they work. Only when understanding is established is it possible to find new ways of working together. Interaction between the various disciplines is complex, and most breakdowns in co-operation are due to misunderstandings and lack of information.

Sometimes nurses will act as representatives of staff organisations. On these occasions there is often a dual rôle, since the presence of the nurse can be a source of reconciliation when misunderstandings arise. Determination to put the needs of patients before other considerations can be a guiding influence to those who may be tempted to take strong measures because they have a grievance. Listening to the problems of other members of the staff influences attitudes, and leads to constructive suggestions for better working relationships. Perhaps it is because of their large numbers, but it is a fact that nurses who adopt a positive approach to problems can have a profound effect on the environment in which they work, and lift the morale of other workers. Conversely the pessimistic nurse with negative views can have a destructive influence, particularly in times of special difficulty.

Committee membership

The number of meetings held seems to be continually on the increase. Perhaps the best contribution the nurse can make when called to attend, is to make sure that the meeting is really necessary. A few tactful questions may reveal that the matter could be solved another way. It is a good idea to assess the cost of bringing people together both in terms of time and money. If this were to be done more often there might be second thoughts about whether the contents of some agenda justify a meeting.

There are however informal meetings which are essential for interchange of information, and proper planning of patient care such as the meeting of the Primary Care Team, which is vital if communications between the members are to be effective. Wherever groups of professionals are working together there needs to be a pattern for sharing their activities. It may be a weekly meeting in operating theatres, or a meeting in the factory, but the establishment of routine contact of this kind is helpful in maintaining good relationships and ensuring uniform objectives for patient care.

Explanations about formal committee procedure can be found in textbooks on management, so the following paragraphs will concentrate on how nurses influence decisions on policy and their daily work, by equipping themselves to be responsible participants at any kind of meeting.

In an amusing article in *The Observer*[5] Katherine Whitehorn described ten types of person who attend meetings. Among them was the 'Train-catcher' who arrives late, makes a commotion and rushes off before the end of the meeting. There is also the 'Damper' who waits until everyone has had their say and then has a good reason why the proposal will not work – but has no suggested alternatives. These characters have been extracted from the list because they illustrate the absence of two of the most vital attributes of a good committee member, courtesy and positive thinking. Even if there is disagreement there is never an excuse for discourtesy.

Positive thinking means concentration on achieving the objectives so that time is not wasted on irrelevant matters. This makes it imperative that each member is absolutely sure about the purpose of the meeting. The preparation to be done beforehand is often exacting, but must be done with proper care and attention. The excuse that there was no time to read the papers is unacceptable.

The good chairman ensures that everyone who has a contribution to make is able to do so. Often nurses do have something to offer, but are reticent to speak, particularly if there is a more senior nurse present. Speaking in public is not easy, but it cannot be left to the few. Most nurses at some time in their career will have to prepare a succinct and reasoned argument both orally and in writing, which will convince others and stand up to questioning. The ability to do this comes with practice, and by taking note of the way other people are successful in putting forward their points of view.

Sometimes nurses are criticised for being emotive when presenting a case which they think will benefit patients. This is possibly because they see the situation primarily in human terms. This viewpoint is not always shared by those not directly involved with patients. For them the economic or administrative issues may be of more importance. On these occasions, having given the facts and supportive statements, it is better to 'stand back' so that questions can be answered calmly and objectively. Willingness to consider alternatives does not necessarily mean that the initial proposal will not ultimately prove to be the right one. If there is a tense atmosphere, the well chosen comment which reveals a sense of humour can often be more effective than prolonged discussion, providing it is said at the right time and with goodwill.

The influence nurses have on fellow members of a group will depend greatly on the amount of concentration that they give to the matters being discussed. It may seem that certain items are irrelevant, and therefore can provide an opportunity to let thoughts wander. This is often just the occasion when the nursing involvement which seemed so remote becomes a major issue. The nurse may be called upon to give her views, and is quite unprepared. To the rest of the meeting this can appear as lack of interest in their affairs. If nurses wish people outside the profession to be concerned about nursing matters, they must also give attention to those issues in which they are not actively engaged, but which still have an indirect effect on patient care.

References

1   Peters, R. S. 1964. *Education as Initiation*. London: Evans.
2   Wilson, M. 1974. 'Wider Requirements in Nursing Education.' Paper given at a conference on 'Wider Issues in Nursing Education', Queen's College, Birmingham, 4–6 January. (Selected conference papers published by the Institute of Religion and Medicine.)
3   *Training in Counselling – a Directory*. 1975. The British Association for Counselling.
4   Meleis, A. I. 1980. Model for establishment of educational programmes in developing countries – the nursing paradoxes in Kuwait. *Journal of Advanced Nursing*, May.
5   Whitehorn, K. 1980. *The Observer*, 11 May.

The Universal Common Aim

Relevance for nursing

"Do you have a Path Lab?" "No, but the fluid was clear when I held it up to the light."[1]

This was the reply of a Dutch nun working in Dagua, Papua New Guinea, who was caring for a child with cerebral malaria. She had carefully diagnosed and treated the child, having performed a lumbar puncture.

When considering a common aim for nurses, it may seem easier to search for those aspects of nursing which are not shared universally for there seem to be so many differences. It may seem unthinkable to some nurses to care for a very sick child with cerebral malaria without laboratory facilities, but this is only an outward sign of socio-economic differences. The universality of nursing need remains paramount.

The World Health Organisation has stated that the health of all peoples is fundamental to the attainment of peace and security.[2] The common aim, therefore, goes beyond the concept of achieving a state of health as an end in itself, and links this with the right of individuals to live in an equable and peaceful environment. Thus the estimation of the quality of life becomes an integral part of the assessment of human need, and cannot be disassociated from the attainment of health.

At the meeting of the International Council of Nurses in Nairobi in 1979, statements were made about the rights of children to be protected from abuse, and the rights of all human beings to effective health care. But there is evidence that 80 per cent of the world's population have no primary health coverage. If the common aim is to become a reality, health programmes of the future must take such matters into consideration rather than proceed in isolation. If planning is to be effective it requires the combined efforts of sociologist, nutritionist and technologist, as well as the doctors and nurses, to make sure that in designing health services, the social and cultural factors are not overlooked.

The composition

Not only do cultural and religious factors influence outlook on health, but also the immediate surroundings. This can form a base line in one situation which is far superior to that in another, so that estimation of what is considered a satisfactory living standard becomes distorted. The quality of life is a relative concept. Some people feel deprived if they are without a refrigerator and a car, whilst for others deprivation means lack of friends and congenial work. What must be recognised is the link between material poverty and ill-health and disablement, and the consequent risks of unemployment. Socio-economic factors also determine the pattern of hygiene, and without a healthy environment, it is difficult to be productive and supply the needs of daily living.

There are plenty of examples of a sequence of events of this kind, particularly in the less fortunate countries. Sometimes a situation of prosperity is reversed because of a major disaster. It is difficult for people in Britain to visualise the havoc caused by a hurricane, and yet in August 1980 when Hurricane David struck Dominica, out of

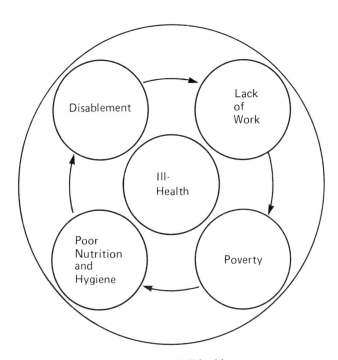

Fig 11.1   The link between poverty and ill health

a population of 85 000, 60 000 of the islanders became homeless. Only a few weeks later Hurricane Allen wiped out 75 per cent of the banana crop of the little island of St Lucia and threatened its economic survival.

Economic viability is not the only important factor in estimating standards of healthy living: the existence of educational opportunities is equally significant. The degree to which people can assume responsibility for their own health depends largely on educational programmes and the degree of response. Shortages of teachers can be a problem, but excellent teaching manuals are available, such as those produced by the League of Red Cross Societies.[3]

Florence Nightingale considered that the laws of health and nursing are one.[4] It may be helpful therefore to take a fresh look at what can be termed 'the laws of nursing' in the form of a code of practice. To do this it is necessary to identify those areas to which nurses endeavour to give precedence on a universal basis.

The Laws of Nursing

A Suggested Code of Practice

1   Nurses strive to promote the greatest degree of well-being for the individual 'patient' and his family, which is attainable under the prevailing circumstances.

2   Nurses when giving care, recognise the need for psychological and spiritual support as well as physical help.

3   Nurses give prime attention to administering safe care, so that their patients come to no harm.

4   Nurses maintain the dignity of human beings, and recognise their right to make their own decisions and be independent.

The reader should refer to the introduction of this book (p. 3) which shows the close relationship between such a code and the philosophy for nursing which has been defined. There may appear to be over-simplification, but when attempting to put these four concepts into action it is apparent that a code of practice cannot be separated from a philosophy for caring, and that ethical considerations are also inherent in the decisions which must be made. It is significant that the International Council of Nurses has taken the lead and given guidelines to the profession regarding ethical conduct. The Council constantly stresses the importance of considering the ethical implications of changes in medical practice and the values held by society.

The interpretation

In trying to interpret the ideals of the common aim, and to follow a code of practice such as has been outlined, nurses will often meet problems which are beyond their control. Modern society has created many of the difficulties and people have become the victims of their own environment and behaviour. This is recognised when considering the effect of mechanisation and speed, and the stress which this can cause. Accident rates and the possibility of cardiac disease are increased. Violence and political unrest are part of life, and they in turn create problems of ill-health, homelessness and grief. Even the environment itself is not free from disturbance, we need to heed the warnings of ecologists and conservationists.

This may seem a gloomy picture, and will not encourage the enthusiastic nurse striving to maintain health and a quality of life for those needing nursing care. There is however something positive which can be done. Members of the health care teams can make sure that they learn more about people and their environment in order to make sense of the pattern of disease. It is not lack of vaccine which inhibits the irradication of some diseases, but a lack of sanitary engineers. In order to nurture healthy children the population has to be of a size comparable with the food supply. Lowering the infant mortality rate is no good if the children die of malnutrition by the time they reach school age.

Nurses in the more affluent parts of the world may consider these thoughts of little relevance to their particular role. However, swift communication and the influence of the media, make it no longer possible, nor right, to ignore them. Many of the problems throughout the world are common to us all, but they vary in intensity. The difficulties in establishing a 'phone in' system for diabetics in a city in Britain, cannot be compared with the problem of establishing effective communication for the Flying Doctor Service in Australia, although the underlying challenge of making contact is the same.

If nurses profess universal aims they must also recognise that there are universal problems and take their part in helping to solve them.

The extent to which nurses can make their voices heard is variable. In Europe 50 per cent of all nursing schools are under medical control. Whilst nurse managers in this country may complain about the extent of the demands made upon them, one Chief Nurse in one of the African states may be expected to provide a nursing service for five million people.

It is anomalies such as these which make the task of solving problems so formidable. However, it has to be done and the summary in the next section may be helpful. It provides examples of some of the activities to which nurses must give their attention in order to achieve universal aims and abide by 'the laws of nursing'.

Implementation of the Common Aim
Action Required

Aim	*Action*
1 *The Establishment of Recognised Standards for Nursing*	a) Identification of a level of nursing competence comparable with the achievement of the objectives contained in nursing care plans.
	b) A continuing review of nursing practice by means of research, and the application of the results of research toward improvements in nursing care.
	c) A recognised pattern of continuing education for all qualified nurses throughout their careers which has proper financial backing.
2 *Recognition of the Extended Role of the Nurse.*	Assessment of the degree to which nurses in varying situations must extend their role to meet human need. Their function is however, primarily that of nursing. In exceptional circumstances it may be necessary for them to assume the function of other professions temporarily. In every case nurses must be competent to carry out their extended role, and willing to assume accountability for their actions with the agreement of their employing authority.
3 *Legal Protection of the Title 'Nurse'.*	a) The establishment of a means of legal control to protect the identity of the qualified nurse, and a procedure for maintaining professional discipline appropriate to that title.
	b) Assessment of the content and 'balance' of the nursing team in every circumstance and the es-

4 *Promotion of the Relevance of the Nursing Ethic.*

   tablishment of suitable training for auxiliaries and volunteers. Education of all nurses to enable them to apply the ethics of nursing to their decisions.

5 *Recognition of the Nurse as a Decision-maker.*

a) Preparation of nurses to enable them to consider problems analytically and with knowledge of the relevant socio-economic factors.

b) Education of government departments and public authorities concerning the need for direct access to nursing advice in all aspects of health planning.

6 *Education of the Public toward Self-care.*

a) The promotion of a responsible attitude toward maintaining personal health.

b) Study of the most effective methods to educate families about the content of healthy living.

c) Recognition by nurses of their teaching and enabling role.

7 *Management of Acute Illness and Disasters.*

a) Protection of those at risk to prevent, wherever possible, the onset of acute illness.

b) Reassessment of financial and other resources to provide a realistic balance between the allocation for curative and preventive measures.

The sequel

It is when implementing the ideals embodied in the common aim that its validity is tested. It soon becomes clear that to achieve a measure of universal agreement on the fundamental constituents of nursing care is of increasing importance. It is no longer possible for nurses to work in isolation. The urgency of the call for nursing help in Kampuchea in the summer of 1980 is just one example.

If these ideals are to be implemented, it is inevitable that there must be changes in attitude toward the role of the nurse within the profession. The unquestioning response to instructions which has been nurtured by a hierarchical nursing structure will have to be reconsidered, and replaced by a more democratic environment. There must be room for initiative, and the opportunity for individual nurses to decide what is best in a particular situation.

Such changes inevitably affect the preparation of nurses for their role and this will be considered in Part III. Before proceeding, however, readers may like to think about the answers to the following questions.

1   How can nurses understand more about the life-style of their patients?
2   In what ways can nurses equip themselves to identify the fundamental constituents of acceptable standards of nursing care?
3   What is required to enable nurses to be more adaptable and resourceful and to develop a healthy attitude towards change?
4   If nurses are to be more conversant with teaching skills, how can they become more skilful in recognising opportunities for learning?

References

1   Melten, A. 1980. A day in Dagua. *Nursing Times*, July.
2   *Proceedings of the 27th World Health Assembly.* 1974. London : HMSO.
3   League of Red Cross Societies. 1976. *Healthy Living – Man and his Environment.* Health Education Programme – Nursing, Guide for Instructors.
4   Nightingale, F. 1859. *Notes on Nursing: What it is and What it is not.* Editions include Blackie, Glasgow, 1974; Dover, London, 1970 (paperback); Duckworth, London, 1970 (facsimile).

PART III

The Way Ahead

12

Reality Defined

Who is the nurse?

In trying to find the answer to the initial question in the preface of this book — What should nurses achieve? — the broad spectrum of their activities has been explored in relation to the needs of individuals within society. The goal nurses should be seeking is the satisfaction of those needs; otherwise how can the existence of nursing as a profession be justified?

It has been shown that in future, the type of nurse required may differ from the nurse of previous images and assumptions. New skills are necessary, and the emphasis is on nurses making decisions about nursing care which previously they have appeared to be content to leave to others. If nurses are accountable for those decisions, they must be conversant with the wider issues which are relevant to their nursing function. This new role also embraces different qualities of leadership. Those in authority have to learn to delegate matters which they have previously controlled. They must be prepared to set the scene for those who are giving care, providing them with tools for the job and support when doing it, and then to stand back.

Who then is this nurse? Having considered the function, what are the qualities which are significant within the nurse's role? It is certain that nurses cannot be defined in terms of knowledge and experience alone. For this reason, the following description is a three-dimensional one, embracing attitudes as well as attributes. Although the description refers to the registered nurse, the issue of the present two-tier system has not been evaded. It may be that there is a place for two grades of qualified nurse within the team, but whatever the decision, it is essential that the person to whom care is delegated has the necessary training and expertise to perform a particular role. Serious problems arise when this important factor is ignored and there is indiscriminate interchange of roles at different levels of the nursing hierarchy.

Profile of the Nurse

A 'portrait' based on the observations and conclusions of Parts I and II – the nurse whom society needs.

Attitudes	Attributes and Abilities	Associated Knowledge
Responsive to feelings of others – is compassionate and caring.	Has developed powers of observation and can use them intelligently and imaginatively.	Understands the stages of human development and the associated physical, psychological and spiritual needs for personal fulfilment and health. Understands the causes of ill-health – has knowledge of the prevention and treatment of disease.
Recognises the uniqueness and dignity of the individual within his/her own environment.	Can analyse information – identify what is relevant and the order of priorities. Can assess the problems and specific needs of those seeking help.	Has acquired skills of listening, is articulate and can communicate effectively verbally and in writing. Has acquired social skills necessary for good relationships. Can think constructively and discriminate. Can apply the theory of decision-making to advantage.
Is committed to nursing objectives and sees these as a shared venture with the patient. Respects opinions and expertise of others.	Is able to obtain the co-operation of the patient and family in deciding short, medium and long-term objectives with a view to preparing a nursing plan.	Has studied the ways in which good relationships can be accomplished and maintained. Knows how to draw on experience and resources available in order to solve problems. Can prepare a nursing plan.

Attitudes	Attributes and Abilities	Associated Knowledge
Is conscientious and believes in professional values and objectives.	Is a safe practitioner — can determine acceptable standards and strives to improve them. Has integrity; can be trusted.	Is conversant with the ethical and legal issues relevant to nursing. Knows the policies, philosophy and objectives of the organisation in which he or she is employed. Understands the meaning of accountability and the implications.
Has a dynamic approach and welcomes responsibility. Can exercise self-discipline in attitudes toward work and in associating with others.	Can assume effectively responsibility for the nursing care of a group of patients — also for families and staff. Is able to fulfil their expectations and needs by assisting, supporting and enabling.	Has the skill and knowledge to make decisions about nursing and implement care plans. Understands the function of a leader, and the right use of power and authority. Can motivate toward agreed goals.
Has a stable outlook and a positive approach to difficult situations.	Can handle complex and stressful situations with poise and assurance. Will take control in a crisis if necessary. Is self-confident but knows when to seek help.	Has knowledge of emergency procedures and how to implement and update them. Understands the function of the multidisciplinary team.

Has a positive attitude and considers a questioning approach an essential part of nursing.	Can innovate, appraise and adapt. Can apply results of evaluation usefully. Is able to prepare and pursue a simple fact-finding project and apply the results to improve nursing care.	Has studied the importance of applying new technology with discretion. Understands the principles of research, the methods used and their application. Is conversant with the appraisal of nursing plans, programmes and performance.
Believes in the necessity to pass on knowledge and skills.	Can recognize learning opportunities and use them effectively for the benefit of others.	Has acquired teaching and learning skills. Knows how to make the best use of available resources.
Is willing to pursue a better understanding of self and strive for personal development. Sees this as an individual responsibility.	Is able to benefit from experience, self-appraisal and new knowledge. Can determine a programme for self-development with guidance and support – set targets and achieve them.	Is aware of opportunities for continuing education, and knows how to plan for personal needs and those of others, to achieve professional growth and maturity.
Has a regard for the property of others, and the importance of 'good house-keeping'.	Uses resources with discretion to avoid waste. Maintains equipment in good order so that safe care can be given and nursing standards maintained.	Understands the financing of the Health Service with particular reference to local needs. Is conversant with local arrangements for the care of patients' property. Understands the ordering procedures and how to obtain maintenance services.

The nurse of the future

Some readers may consider that there is nothing new in the content of the profile. This will be because most of the qualities and attitudes which have been included have previously been taken for granted. It is assumed that they exist in the 'make-up' of potential nurses and develop almost by instinct. However the emphasis on these personal qualities may necessitate a more radical change in thinking among members of the profession than is at first apparent. There is a misconception that if new ways of working and fresh attitudes are introduced into the educational programme, changes will inevitably follow in the practice of nursing. This is far from the truth. Changes have to be made throughout the organisation, and once established, have to be sustained and evaluated. This implies commitment and the readiness to allow nurses to develop as people. It is necessary to share humbly and graciously what individual nurses have to offer, using their strengths. There are centres of excellence in large cities and in the small communities. It is is from these centres that there has to be a 'reaching out' and an extension of what has already been achieved, so that others may accept what is offered, and learn. This learning process need not be confined to Britain. With the links which have been established within the European Economic Community, and with the Third World, there are opportunities for sharing experiences such as have never been possible before. Brian Kay, writing about a study period spent in Holland observing the care of the profoundly handicapped, noted that we have much to learn about concepts of mobility, occupation, and creativity from our neighbours in the Netherlands. He found that we also have something to offer, especially in the field of basic nursing care and professional identification.[1]

For this kind of sharing to be effective, it is essential to understand the true meaning of status and power. Status is earned, and is based on mutual respect. Power is only effective when there is influence *with* people, and not power over them.[2]

References

1   Kay, B. 1981. Care of the profoundly handicapped in the Netherlands. *Nursing Times*, 9 April, p. 655.
2   Metcalfe, H. C. and Urwick, L (Eds). 1941. *Dynamic Administration — the collected papers of Mary Parker Follett*. London: Pitman.

13
Education and Preparation

The essence of education

The chief aim of nursing education is to prepare people who will meet effectively the needs of those requiring care. Previous chapters have discussed some of these needs and have emphasised that they are ever-changing. In the foreword of 'Patients First'[1] the Secretary of State for Social Services reminds readers that

> we must never forget that it is people not organisations who have the care and cure of patients in their charge. Just as the needs of patients will change over the years, so will the needs of those who care for them.

The nursing educational programme must therefore be adaptable. However, a close look at the nursing profile on p. 101 confirms that there is a certain content of professional nursing which does not change. This is particularly so when considering the attributes of the registered nurse. These are fundamental to nursing of quality and therefore require emphasis in the preparatory period.

Before discussing priorities, it is essential to be clear about objectives. Everyone who participates in nursing education must be agreed about the role of the nurse; only then can preparation for that role be pursued with a shared philosophy and the same vision. It is essential that there is harmony between those in the nursing service and within nursing education, and that they have confidence in one another. Policies will then enable objectives to be realised, and the student nurses will understand what *being* a nurse really entails by the examples given not only by the staff of the educational centre but also those in the service areas.

It is important that an understanding of the content of nursing is conveyed at an early stage. So often recruitment brochures show what nurses do, and give an indication of training opportunities, but fail to describe what will be asked of the nurse as a person, once qualified. Unless this information is available, potential recruits cannot compare their attitudes and life-style with what will eventually be required of them. This raises the question of the difference between entering a profession and doing a job. It is also essential that those who wish to become nurses can link their ideals and aspirations with the philosophy of the Nursing School so that motivation is maintained and stimulated.

Continuity with general education

It was Goethe who said 'he who moves not forward – goes backward.' There must be a logical progression linking school and community life. In a BBC Television series entitled 'The Living City'[2] the children in a city school made a plea to their teachers for more opportunity to make their own decisions, and to exercise leadership. They commented that just choosing a particular job, and then learning the skills, or passing the required examinations, restricted their ability to understand the demands of the world beyond school.

General education could be more closely associated with that of nursing, if, as well as careers talks, there were short-term interchanges of teaching staff. It would then be possible to share at first hand what is needed by those who choose a career which predominantly involves communicating with others. Some schools are doing enterprising work such as encouraging the children to produce their own radio programmes, but for some the first test of expressing themselves to strangers is when they attend for an interview for their first job. If more attention could be given to helping young people to understand the complexity of making good relationships, and acquiring skills of verbal as well as written communication, it would also prepare them to take their part more fully in modern society.

With the foundations of effective communication firmly laid during the years at school, it would be possible to build on this on entering nursing, and allow a natural expansion of knowledge as the nursing student comes into contact with patients, their families and other members of the caring team. Continuity of learning of this kind has many advantages, and it would be possible to provide progressive education along the following lines as an integral part of nursing.

Foundations for professional life

What follows is not an attempt to revise the curriculum for nursing education – this is a task for experts, but suggestions for changes in

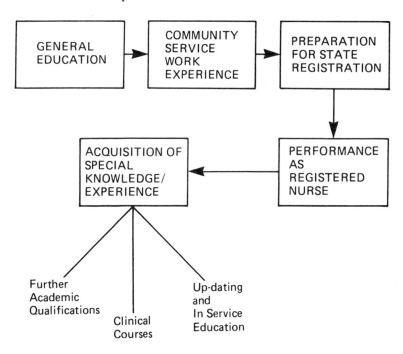

Fig 13.1 Progressive nursing education

emphasis which will be necessary if the profile of the nurse which has been outlined is to become a reality.

Any fresh approach to the management of patient care not only necessitates reconsideration of the educational programme, but also of the manner in which clinical experience is obtained. With the apprentice-type system a considerable amount of learning takes place almost subconsciously by exposure to certain situations. It is some of these 'hidden' aspects of learning which need to be acquired in a more conscious and constructive way. This is particularly so where the development of the nurse-patient relationship is concerned. One reason why former methods of learning no longer suffice, is that patients are discharged early and that not only are they in hospital for a shorter time, but they are not in bed! This makes it harder for nurses in training to model themselves on the performance of senior staff who may be with ambulant patients or obscured by the walls and partitions of newly designed wards.

Pressure to include new material in the curriculum and to offer nurses practical experience in a wider variety of specialities, makes it imperative to re-think the foundations of nursing education. It is necessary to concentrate more on principles and on helping student nurses to apply them in different situations. For example, when learning the principles of the nursing care for a patient having surgery, the possible problems, including psychological implications such as a changed body image, can be applied to the care of someone having an amputation of a limb, or a woman having a hysterectomy. In the past, the study of nursing has been divided into compartments by the medical diagnosis and the type of ward in which the patient resides. As a result, general or arterial surgery and gynaecology are considered as separate within nursing education in spite of the fact that there is much which is common to them all. The aim must be to teach student nurses to analyse, discriminate, and make decisions in relation to individual patients, applying their nursing knowledge to the total situation and not limiting this to the medical diagnosis.

Applying principles of nursing over a broad spectrum in this way, entails the most careful supervision during the learning period to ensure safe practice. The advantage is that it allows more opportunity to concentrate on the planning of nursing care and to identify and solve both actual and potential problems. These thoughts have been illustrated in Figs 13.2 and 13.3. Fig 13.2 shows some of the pitfalls of the present situation. Fig 13.3 makes suggestions for change in emphasis.

The priorities

Fig 13.3 gives an indication of the priorities in preparing nurses for state registration, and for becoming members of a profession. The success of a plan of this kind depends on the co-operation and understanding of patients and their families, and other members of the caring team, who play a large part in helping the students to learn. Skills in building relationships and in communication are therefore a priority and need to be acquired at the earliest opportunity. Student nurses must also recognise the essentials of good teamwork. They will discover that successful membership of a team requires a readiness to relinquish authority if a more appropriate person is required as leader in a particular situation. It may not always be the doctor or the nurse, it may be the social worker, or it could be the patient.

The ability to assess, analyse and solve problems is dependent on skills of observation and recognition. These cannot be learnt in short sessions labelled 'Preparation for Management'. They are an integral

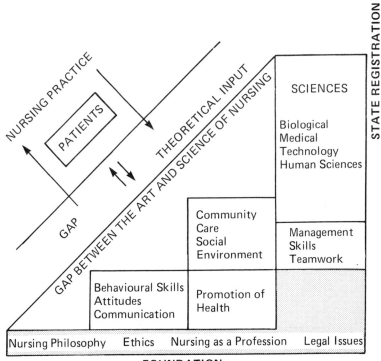

SCIENCES

Biological
Medical
Technology
Human Sciences

Community
Care
Social
Environment

Management
Skills
Teamwork

Behavioural Skills
Attitudes
Communication

Promotion of
Health

Nursing Philosophy   Ethics   Nursing as a Profession   Legal Issues

FOUNDATION

Notes

a) Learning is fragmented as subject matter is isolated in sections.

b) There is a gap between theory and practice.

c) Emphasis on medical sciences and disease.

d) Gap between art and science of nursing.

e) Low priority given to professional nursing issues and communications.

f) Decision-making as a specific entity does not feature.

Fig 13.2   Nursing education (foundation and emphasis) – present situation'

part of all aspects of nursing and include the use of resources so that there can be safe practice and acceptable standards of care. In the process nurses will need help to understand that professional commitment can produce conflict with other concepts such as those connected with industrial relations. However, if priority is given to professional competence, the nursing student will be able to form

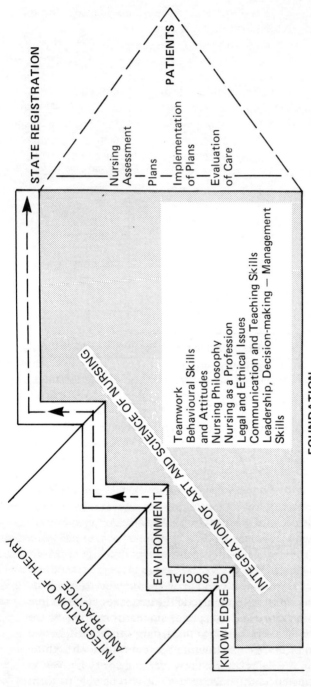

STATE REGISTRATION

PATIENTS

Nursing Assessment

Plans

Implementation of Plans

Evaluation of Care

INTEGRATION OF ART AND SCIENCE OF NURSING

Teamwork
Behavioural Skills and Attitudes
Nursing Philosophy
Nursing as a Profession
Legal and Ethical Issues
Communication and Teaching Skills
Leadership, Decision-making — Management Skills

FOUNDATION

INTEGRATION OF THEORY AND PRACTICE

ENVIRONMENT

OF SOCIAL

KNOWLEDGE

Notes

a) High priority to nursing aspects—broadening out from the foundation.

b) Extension of subject matter concurrently with nursing issues.

c) Integration of theory and practice.

d) Integration of art and science of nursing.

convictions about what is right and wrong, and identify those rewards in nursing which bring satisfaction.

The list of priorities therefore could look something like this:

- The content of making decisions.
- Communication and behavioural skills.
- The essentials of teamwork.
- Leadership as the means of enabling others to reach their objectives.
- Analytical skills, and the recognition of problems.
- The essentials of safe practice to ensure the best possible standards of nursing care.

The learning environment

All who are involved in the educational programme have a responsibility to provide an environment conducive to learning. Recent research[3] has given some indication about the nature of what is termed 'a high student-orientated ward'. It was found that there was a direct relationship between those factors which student nurses consider to be important for learning, and their satisfaction with nursing generally. The latter appeared to be dependent on the ward atmosphere, which in turn, was determined by the ward sister as the key person. The most satisfactory situation was one where there was good teamwork, where communications were effective, and where the ward sister would spare time to listen to problems. Time was given to teaching and to making the maximum use of learning opportunities. Before making decisions, the sister would feel it appropriate to discuss with her subordinates.

This brief account of the findings, confirms that there is a firm obligation on the part of the leaders in the clinical areas to create a climate where questions can be asked without fear, and where there is acknowledgement of work well done. It is sometimes anxiety on the part of senior nursing staff which makes them quick to criticise, since they anticipate possible errors. It is not always remembered that if adequate teaching has been given, students will respond to being trusted. This emphasises the need for at least one member of the nursing team to have attended a recognised course in teaching methods and skills. Those concerned must have a personal commitment and desire to be involved in the education of nurses, and enjoy this participation.

The goals which the student nurse wishes to achieve have to be shared with the ward or community nursing sister, and the learning objectives agreed with the staff of the School of Nursing, who then truly become members of a team. The achievement of these objectives becomes a shared responsibility, requiring regular assessment of success. How this is done requires further investigation, but one of the essentials is agreement between those in nursing education and the service on the standards which are acceptable. Any event or policy which influences standards of nursing must be jointly scrutinised so that changes within the learning environment progress smoothly and enhance the preparation of nurses rather than impeding it.

Some indication of the effectiveness of learning can be obtained from reports on the student nurse, providing the assessment is fair, and not a reflection of the assessor's particular prejudices. Although much hard work was done to introduce the King's Fund Assessment Forms which are widely used, they are now out of date. The concept of the student nurse as a 'pair of hands' is reinforced in the first section:

1   *Application to work*

1   Exceptionally industrious.
    A very keen and willing worker.

5   Consistently prompt in carrying out duties.

Whilst it is important that work is undertaken conscientiously and that duties are done promptly, the prominence given to these statements tends to detract from the concept of a student nurse as someone gaining experience in a learning capacity.

In a subsequent section comments on performance are separated from attitude to patients and to colleagues. The problem is that there is no clarification of the words which are used. For example in Section II No. 6. 'Maintains very high standards when carrying out nursing procedures.' 'High standards' can be assessed in different ways, and the performance of a procedure may be technically correct, but ignore the needs of the patients. Now that learning objectives are being formulated as part of the assessment of progress in many Schools of Nursing, this kind of appraisal is no longer appropriate. Where the State Final Examination has been replaced by an internal and continuous assessment, the student has the opportunity to reach goals which have been determined objectively and to a specific standard.

Learning opportunities

In case the impression has been given that learning only occurs in clinical areas, it should be stated that any situation which enhances the development of the nurse can be of value so long as there are defined objectives. The broad base of inter-related learning illustrated in Fig. 13.3 shows that there is a continuous build up of knowledge related to professional nursing. For this to be successful, those who teach must develop their ability to recognise and grasp learning opportunities, and weld them together. This is best understood by an example. Suppose that the learning objective is to help the student nurse to understand the meaning of teamwork and the importance of co-ordinating the contribution of the various professionals. The visit of the hospital Chaplain could be the 'learning opportunity'. A discussion with the Chaplain will invariably have taken place in the School of Nursing, but the students may only have theoretical knowledge of his role and function, and there have probably been few opportunities to consider their relationship with him as a member of the team. It is important that this should have been considered constructively if nurses are to make the right decisions. It may be helpful to look at the following situations which could occur, and the lessons to be learnt.

Situation	*Learning Opportunity*
The patient says he wishes to discuss a domestic matter which is worrying him, and impeding progress. He asks to see the Chaplain rather than the social worker as the nurse has suggested.	The nursing student can be helped to understand that the patient's wishes must be gratified, regardless of personal views about the choice of helper.
A little boy has diabetes, and thinks it is because he stole some sweets. An adult patient feels guilty that he has precipitated his illness.	By discussion to show how children perceive in the early days of maturity, and that they have need for spiritual support as well as adults. To demonstrate how comfort can be obtained.
'Why has this happened to me?' A question which may be asked of the nurse.	To assist nursing students to look at their own attitudes to suffering, so that they can make an honest and supportive answer by reason of their own philosophy and belief. To point out that the Chaplain is someone with whom such questions can be shared.

During the discussion with the nursing students questions may arise about sharing the objectives of the nursing plan with the Chaplain.

Student nurses can be helped to identify those circumstances when the care of the patient will be enhanced by the involvement of the Chaplain, and why.

In this last situation the art of discrimination is being taught, and the learner has an opportunity to distinguish situations which are comparable, and those which are not.

Teaching on these lines depends on the closest co-operation with colleagues, so that there is no overlap, and to ensure that essentials are not omitted. It is team teaching at its best, and is well worth pursuing.

Who teaches?

Many nurses consider that they cannot pass on their knowledge 'because they are no good at teaching'. This is often due to a misconception of the content of teaching. The example given in the previous section is intended to show the extent of learning opportunities, but these may not occur simultaneously – nor may it be feasible to spend the time which is required to cover the total situation. However, what matters is the recognition that to teach does not necessarily mean that a formal session must be arranged which is devoted to one specific topic. So often, such sessions are restricted to the giving of information, with little involvement of the learners; whereas the effective teacher grasps each opportunity as it arises, to reveal what is currently happening, and to enable the learners to gain insight, and to understand the need to correlate their knowledge.

Some of the most effective teaching is done by those, whoever they may be, who set an example by their own good practice, and remember to bring to the learners' attention what to anticipate and observe during their nursing care. This is a valuable way of passing on knowledge and experience but needs to be extended to what nurses say to their patients and the relatives. There are many students of nursing who have grave anxieties about how to talk with patients, particularly the dying,[4] but they do not know how to gain this knowledge. Much help could be given if the sister/charge nurse or staff nurses returning from an interview or from answering the telephone, would explain what they said and why. Building up a 'reference' store of this nature enables students to acquire confidence, and equips them for this difficult task. Although no two circumstances are alike, they will have valuable experience on which to draw.

There will be those who will argue that to teach in this way is unrealistic amid the pressures of a busy ward, or on the district. And yet most of those who put forward such views would be the first to confirm that nursing is best learnt beside the patient. What then is the answer? One suggestion might be that where there are two sisters or charge nurses working on a ward, one of them should be designated specifically for teaching. This would entail assuming responsibility for the implementation of the educational programme. Working closely with the nurse teachers, it should be possible by this means to provide continuity of learning, and to meet the requirements of individual students.

Some ward and community sisters are attending short courses in the art of teaching. In future, however, this should be an essential part of their preparation if learning is to be a progressive activity, and not be confined to statutory courses.

A self-directed programme

As nurses help themselves to learn, they can identify their special needs, and also appreciate the requirements of others. By acting out the role of patient, they can, for example, feel what it is like to be incapacitated. Lying flat in bed can produce many problems, and the learner who looks at the situation with fresh eyes may produce some very practical suggestions for solving them.

Finding opportunities to gain and apply knowledge not only helps students to develop themselves as people, but makes learning exciting and rewarding. Personal responsibility for achieving goals throughout the preparatory period means that this attitude toward education is established, and becomes the natural order of things once registration is reached.

References

1 *Patients First: Consultative paper on the Structure and Management of the National Health Service in England and Wales.* 1979. London: HMSO.

2 'The Living City.' Weekly BBC Television series, Autumn 1980.

3 Orton, H. D. 1981. *Ward Learning Climate and Student Nurse Response.* London: Rcn.
4 Hooper, J. E. 1981. Geriatric patients and nurse learner's attitudes. 1981. *Nursing Times Occasional Papers*, 26 March, Vol. 77, No. 10.

14

Growth to Maturity

The previous chapter has shown that it is possible to establish the foundations for continuing education within the student nurse's initial programme. Registration as a qualified nurse then becomes the *beginning* of true professional growth. Progress towards maturity means that there is a gradual development of potential for a purpose. It implies being prepared for the fulfilment of personal desires as well as the demands of others. In a recent book describing the application of the nursing process to the nursing care of senior

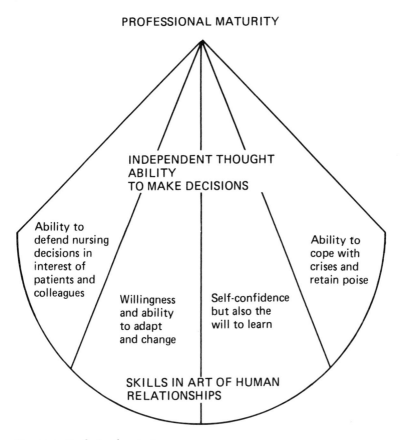

PROFESSIONAL MATURITY

INDEPENDENT THOUGHT
ABILITY
TO MAKE DECISIONS

Ability to
defend nursing
decisions in
interest of
patients and
colleagues

Ability to
cope with
crises and
retain poise

Willingness
and ability
to adapt
and change

Self-confidence
but also the
will to learn

SKILLS IN ART OF HUMAN
RELATIONSHIPS

Fig 14.1 Professional maturity

citizens,[1] maturity is conceived as a combination of biological, psychological and social age. In this context biological age refers to the stage of development within the physiological process and life span. Psychological age is the person's ability to adapt to his environment; this includes such things as perceptual ability, learning, problem-solving and the development of personality. Social age is the degree to which there is involvement in human relationships at work, at home and within the community, and also the individual's ability to fulfil the expectations of others. It is possible to identify the development of the nurse within these areas.

Freedom, responsibility and independence

It is not surprising that, in attempting to come to terms with the changing attitudes of society and the needs of health care, that nurses have been uncertain of their responsibilities. However, professional maturity depends on an understanding of the relationship between responsibility and personal freedom. The correct balance has to be acquired. To this must be added the capacity for independent thought. To be able to weigh up a situation, and make a wise and conscientious decision, is part of being responsible; but this also includes being prepared to accept the consequences for the action that follows. This is the true meaning of accountability.

Freedom	*Responsibility*	*Independence*
Opportunity to make choices.	Willingness to accept results of one's actions.	Independent thought
Appreciation of the limits of the environment.	Respect for human dignity and consideration for others.	Personal values which can be explained.
Acceptance of authority of government and the law.	Willingness to satisfy the objectives of the profession and the employing authority and abide by their policy.	Ability to do an effective job and maintain standards.
Freedom from prejudice.	Self-understanding and poise.	Ability to pursue new concepts and evaluate their worth.

These qualities are achieved throughout a professional career at different stages, according to the experience gained and the individual effort of the nurse. Where the goal is directed solely towards status and promotion, some of these attributes may be ignored or overlooked. However, if there is a sincere desire to achieve maximum usefulness to the community, status is usually acquired because it is grounded on respect. Authority is also given because there is trust and confidence in the nurse's judgement.

Continuing education

Chapter 13 gives an outline of a concept of progressive education (p. 107). Table 14.2 shows this in more detail.

Guidance for development

All qualified nurses require a personal development plan, and someone to help them to fulfil it. This will usually be the person next in line, but there need not be any hard and fast rule. During the period as a student nurse, tutors and clinical teachers undertake this task, and there is no reason why in certain circumstances the pattern should not continue where a particularly helpful relationship has been established. The position in the hierarchy should not be the deciding factor, what matters is that there should be mutual respect and trust. For example, it may be that an experienced community or ward sister is the best person to help a colleague new to the job. However, it must be recognised that the people giving guidance have to be equipped to do this, and should aim at enabling the nurses to make their own decisions and recognise their personal needs. Experimentation on these lines might be more fruitful than the present system and produce more enthusiasm for development programmes.

When choosing the most appropriate form of further education, the opportunities within the working environment should not be overlooked. Sometimes the most successful learning takes place in familiar surroundings, where there is active support and encouragement to achieve a particular goal. This is well illustrated in the field of nursing management in a document entitled *Management Development Options in the NHS*.[2] The section on *non-course* options contains twelve listed alternatives. It is made clear that certain criteria have to be fulfilled before off-the-job training can be justified. Among these are situations where the skilled teaching which is required is not available locally, or if time is needed for training to be effective because a change in attitude or social skills is necessary.

Table 14.2 Progressive Nursing Education (II)
The Post-Registration Pattern

Renewal and Refreshment	Retraining and New Knowledge (mainly In-Service)	Formal Education To obtain Further Education or Degree (mainly external)	Evaluation
Assessment of progress Development of aptitudes Identification of deficiencies (Best way to fill gaps) Restatement of personal goals within the overall objectives	Identify priorities Prepare plans Search for means of obtaining new knowledge and skills Set targets	Special Courses academic or clinical content Applied and initiated research	Establish means of assessing progress Compare outcome with target Reassess possibilities
	Applied Experience Research* and project work Reading . . . . . . Visits	These will take place throughout the pattern of continuous education.	

* Research-mindedness i.e. a questioning of established practice — innovation and initiation on the job.

Applying the principles of the nursing process to professional development

Mention has been made of the importance of understanding the principles underlying the construction of a development programme. These can best be defined within the stages of the nursing process.

1 *Assessment*	What are the needs of the individual to fulfil the nurse's role? How can problems which exist be overcome? What are the priorities?
2 *Setting out Objectives and Making the Plan*	What can be achieved within a reasonable time? Goals must be realistic and compatible with the overall objectives of the profession and/or the employing authority.
3 *Implementing the Plan*	Action has to take place. This may mean special facilities, removing obstacles, obtaining the co-operation of others.
4 *Evaluation*	Having agreed targets, they must be achieved on time. Results need to be assessed and adjustment may be required to plans. New goals may emerge.

Advanced education

For nurses to be able to meet the challenge of the many changes which the future will demand, they have to develop their capacity to think with foresight and to broaden their knowledge beyond the confines of nursing itself.

> The aim should be to produce not mere specialists but rather cultivated men and women. It is a distinguishing characteristic of a healthy higher education that even when it is concerned with practical techniques it imparts them on a plane of generality that makes possible their application to many problems.[3]

This aim is sometimes best achieved within a university or polytechnic. It is important that nurses do not feel threatened by what the educational institutions have to offer, but welcome their support. Nurses can best retain the values and the traditions in which they believe, not by withdrawing into a world of their own, but by using their influence and contributing to the interchange of ideas in places of learning. The profession has a distinctive culture and much to offer, but this has to be shared in order that it is understood.

Future leaders require opportunities to develop themselves to capacity. There are various ways in which this can happen, and some may bring unexpected and seemingly irrelevant experience. However in retrospect it is these opportunities which often prove to be the most fruitful, since they provide a better understanding of human relationships, and of society.

The three-fold responsibility

Professional development does not depend only on formal educational experience. Much is learnt by example, and if the environment is right, there is a continuous absorption of new thoughts, so that efforts are made to improve nursing practice. All nurses have a responsibility toward each other to help in this way. This is particularly so where nurses are managing a part of the District, for they have considerable influence on the welfare of their staff and the opportunities provided for extending their skills.

Progress therefore depends on the combined effort of those within the nursing service, within the education field, and the individual nurse. The importance of this co-operation is discussed in the next chapter. Meanwhile it will be helpful to summarise the essentials for progress toward professional maturity.

1   Nurses must have the opportunity to develop their full potential and gain self-confidence to meet the demands of the job.

2   Nurses must be able to use the knowledge they acquire, be able to look critically at current practice and make suggestions for improvement.

3   Facilities should be available to keep up to date with clinical and professional information. There must be access to libraries and opportunity for study.

4   Those who can contribute to nursing literature and research should be enabled to do so.

5   Professional development must primarily benefit those receiv-

ing care, but should also maximise the enjoyment and satisfaction of nursing.

6   Achievement of objectives is a three-fold responsibility.

References

1   Murray, R., Huelskoelter, M. and O'Driscoll, D. 1980. *The Nursing Process in Later Maturity*. London: Prentice Hall.
2   *Management Development Options in the NHS*. Health Services Management Centre Occasional Paper No. 14, University of Birmingham.
3   *Higher Education*. 1963. London: HMSO, Cmnd 2154, Chapter II, Para 26.

15

Framework for Action

Several suggestions have been made to help nurses re-examine their attitudes toward nursing care, and to think constructively about the future. Reference to previous chapters will refresh the reader's mind about the effect of attitudes on the environment (see pp. 61, 111). The broader issues will now be considered, which, although they may appear to be less relevant, have a marked influence on the quality of nursing care.

What's wrong with Salmon?

It could be said that some of the recommendations of the Salmon Committee[1] are now out of date, since periodic review of an organisation is necessary in the light of change. There is a danger that consideration of organisational structures may take precedence, and the underlying principles then fail to be properly interpreted. For example, it was never intended that 'management' should be divorced from 'nursing skills' and be considered as a separate subject, taught in isolation, and then somehow applied on returning to the job. However this has happened in some instances causing conflict and misapprehension. This has been particularly apparent in the case of the nursing officers who have sometimes become the victims of a 'see-saw' effect. One moment they are expected to be fully involved in clinical matters, and the next in supervising a large part of the area in which they work.

The Salmon Committee proposals were that the nursing officers should be able to participate fully in nursing care by actually taking the place of the ward or community sister for a recognised period,

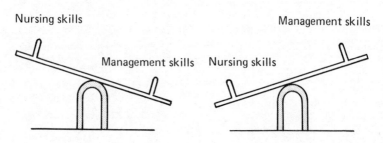

Nursing skills | Management skills

Management skills | Nursing skills

such as the sister's or charge nurse's holiday. Where this has been done the credibility of the nursing officer has not been in doubt and he or she has been recognised as having first hand knowledge of the nursing needs and the problems. The nursing officers have found much satisfaction in this interpretation of their role, which also allows scope for identifying areas where nursing research can improve the quality of care.

There are similar problems to be solved at other levels of the hierarchy. Dr Don White has raised the issue of the conflict between the balance of the District Nursing Officer's role, as both head of a large professional hierarchy and member of a concensus management team.[2] A decision has to be made about the *nursing* content of this post if there is to be good practice throughout the district. The responsibility cannot be entirely delegated, since the District Nursing Officer is ultimately accountable. The head of the nursing service has to be acknowledged, primarily as an expert in nursing. This does not mean he or she has expertise in all specialities, but implies a depth of knowledge and an understanding of people which enables a ready response to their need. This is the substance of good nursing and good management.

Management and nursing skills therefore must be brought together, and the nursing process is proof that the two are interwoven. This unification of the functions of assessment, planning, organisation and evaluation can be demonstrated.[3]

Clinical Nurse	**Nurse Manager**
Assessment	
Observation of the patient/client and his environment.	Observation of staff reactions to policies and objectives. Observation of needs of community – priorities in health care – manpower trends and availability of resources.
Communication skills. Art of listening and interviewing.	Communication skills – art of listening and interviewing.
Collection of facts, identifying priorities.	Collection of facts, identifying priorities.
Planning	
Interpretation in the light of clinical knowledge and the facts.	Interpretation in the light of 'managerial' knowledge and the facts.

Setting short and long-term goals for the patient and his family.

Deciding what to do to solve the problems, keeping in mind quality of care, safe care, and the nursing policies laid down.

Involving the patient and his family in the plan of care, and other disciplines as required, in order that there is co-ordination and progress toward similar goals.

Setting short and long-term goals for the service.

Deciding what to do to solve problems, keeping in mind quality of care, safe care, and revising policies if necessary.

Involving the staff and other disciplines in order that there is co-ordination of planning, and progress toward similar goals.

Implementation
(Organisation)

Setting the plan into action, taking into account:
   The patient's ability to help himself.
   Professional resources.
   Equipment available.

Teaching needs – both of patient family, nursing and other students.

Organising for continuity of care.

Providing team leadership, and an environment in which good work can be done.

Setting the plan into action, taking into account:
   The amount of delegation which can be safely undertaken.
   Professional resources.
   Time available.

Teaching needs – development of staff – orientation of new staff to fulfil their respective roles.

Organising for continuity in providing a service.

Providing leadership of the area of responsibility and an environment in which good work can be done.

Evaluation
(Control)

Analysing results of implementation of plan for patient and family.

Considering changes which have taken place which necessitate reassessment.

Considering quality of care provided, alongside the standards and policies which have been agreed.
   Taking action where needed.*

Identifying areas of nursing practice which require revision of research.
   Communicating the need together with a suggestion for action to appropriate level.

Analysing results of implementation of plan in consultation with those delivering nursing care.

Considering changes which are necessary and the case for re-planning or for adjustment of the plan.

Considering quality of care provided alongside the standards and policies which have been agreed.
   Taking action where needed.

Facilitating clinical nurses and managers to undertake research project and questioning established practice.

Communicating changes in planning which may be required to patient/client, colleagues, and other disciplines.

Communicating changes in planning which may be required to staff and other disciplines.

Misunderstanding of the purpose of the organisational structure has also inhibited the nurse's ability to make decisions. It was intended by the Salmon Committee that the nurse holding a particular place in the hierarchy should not only have responsibility but also authority. Instead, there has often been a tendency to rely on the 'line above' so that the structure becomes a prop instead of a framework for orderliness. In future there will be an increasing emphasis on teamwork and the lateral relationships will assume more importance.

The concept of working in teams necessitates reconsideration of the selection of nurses for all positions of leadership. Personal qualities will be more in evidence, and also the ability to maintain cohesion and enlist co-operation. The present interview system is deficient, and research is required to find more effective ways of assessment.

It would be interesting to take the middle column of the nursing profile pages (pp. 101 – 103) and make the statements into open questions instead of the usual reference. The referee should be asked to give a tangible example in each section to support the comments made. This information could then be supplemented by observation of inter-personal skills in a real-life situation.

Positive attitudes to health

The importance of a change in attitude towards the objectives of the health service has already been stressed, but this more positive approach needs to be extended to nurses themselves and to their place of work. They have an individual obligation to contribute to a healthy environment, and cannot leave this entirely to the Occupational Health Nurse or safety representatives.

As well as physical dangers, there are the hazards of emotional strain. The most effective supervision occurs when the leader has an affinity with the nursing team which enables stress to be sensed at an early stage. The attitude that nurses will always manage somehow, has almost become a status symbol, and all kinds of excuses are made by those in authority to ignore the danger signals. However, there is an inevitable sequence of events if help is not forthcoming. If there are not enough people to do the work, there will be short cuts; this in turn leads to a fall in standards and complaints. The nurses feel they are in a seemingly hopelss situation, and either absent themselves, or become sick. This reduces the numbers further, and reinforces the stress and strain.

It is important that there are rest rooms for those who work in particularly exacting situations, such as where there are patients with severe burns, or who are mutilated. It may be that a break from contact with the patient is required after a comparatively short spell. Nurses and their medical colleagues should not feel guilty about this, and should recognise their own need for emotional support and refreshment. Such situations emphasise the need for a more flexible approach toward the organisation of working hours in other areas, such as where there are mentally handicapped patients or the elderly mentally ill.

There is useful research available into the cause of stress among student nurses,[4] and there are projects under way such as the survey concerning the possible relationship between job stress in nursing and smoking habits.[5] However, since reactions to stressful situations differ so much, it is possible that the common factors which can be identified are few. There is one essential need for all who are exposed

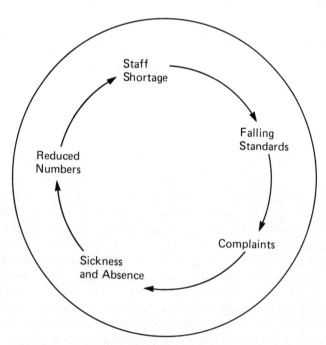

Fig 15.1   Shortage of staff – the vicious circle

to emotional strain, and that is security. The following conversation which took place between a little girl aged three, and her father illustrates this point. She had gone upstairs to undress before going to bed.

> 'Daddy I need your help' . . . 'But why', said her father, 'you know how to undress yourself.' 'Yes' was the reply, 'but sometimes people need people anyway, even if they know how to do things for themselves.' [6]

Consideration of attitudes to health must inevitably bring into question the quality of life for those nurses who, because of illness or disability, cannot continue their careers. Much is said about continuity of care for patients, but where nurses are concerned, it is not uncommon for them to be without professional support at a time when it is most needed. Nurses have a responsibility to make every effort to help find suitable re-employment for their colleagues and to see them through the rehabilitation period and beyond if necessary. There is work to be done to identify suitable occupations and inform the rehabilitation centres accordingly.

Progressive learning in practice

If education is to be continuous throughout a nurse's career, it is no longer practical to divide a district into teaching and non-teaching areas. Those where student nurses are gaining clinical experience will have particular significance, but learning opportunities must be grasped in all situations for the benefit of the various grades of staff. It is therefore imperative that the handing on of skills and knowledge is seen as an essential part of nursing, and not an additional activity to be engaged upon in special circumstances.

The Ward Sister training projects [7] will hopefully have something to offer, to enable potential sisters to appreciate the most effective ways of linking theory with practice. Under the guidance of the Nurse Teacher and Ward Sister Preceptors it should be possible for them ultimately to provide a model which will demonstrate not only how to do the job of nursing, but how to be a nurse.

To make sure that learning does take place it might be useful to set up small 'educational teams' within areas of the nursing service to monitor its effectiveness with the aid of a check list. This would be a kind of peer audit undertaken by representatives of those who teach.

The surveillance of in-service programmes and post-certificate studies could be included.

A closer link between the service areas and the educational centre can be formed by making joint appointments. This was recommended in the Report of the Royal Commission on the Health Service.[8] Appointments of this kind are now being established. The Nurse Teacher concerned holds two contracts of employment, and undertakes sessions in the Education Centre as well as a stated amount of time in the ward in the capacity of sister or charge nurse. This enables the Nurse Teacher to be fully conversant with current nursing practice, and, as the 'sister', to be in a position to share actual nursing problems with colleagues. This exciting combination of activity is possible within the ward or the community and can benefit not only the nurses involved, but also the learners whom they teach. Of great importance is the fact that this scheme can give a most valuable contribution to the care of patients.

Some of the present difficulties in ensuring a continuity of education for qualified nurses stem from lack of planning in the first instance. In-service education is sometimes considered to be well established, and impressive lists of study days are produced, but these do not necessarily meet the requirements of the staff. Initially, a comprehensive survey of the interests and aspirations of the nurses is required, to find out their attitude toward further education. There has to be motivation and an understanding of the need for personal development if in-service programmes are to be of benefit.

Having decided what is necessary, qualified teaching staff, and adequate finance must be available, and considered to be a priority.

Research and the quality of care

It is recognised that if the results of research are properly used they can help nurses to improve the care they give. However, problems arise in finding a satisfactory means of measuring professional social skills and attitudes. Dr Rosemary Crow has suggested that nurses need to develop their capacity to ask the right questions.[9] To do this they need to understand the content of social skills, and be able to identify those which are of particular value in nursing. Many of these are related to the common courtesies which should be an essential part of any relationship which is primarily concerned with the feelings and needs of another person. The fact that this courteous and thoughtful approach is not always apparent is not given sufficient attention. It is impossible to separate social skills from meaningful communication, so the failure may lie in this direction.

Nurses will respond to their patients according to their own experience. It is possible that the warmth which is sometimes lacking can be attributed to working in an environment where they themselves are not treated with understanding. Before attempting any formal research therefore, it is essential to get the working conditions right and to establish an atmosphere where people as individuals matter. Where this atmosphere exists, nurses will feel free to ask questions, and to be themselves. They will find satisfaction in what they do because they will have been made aware of the value of their personal contribution, especially the more reticent members of the nursing team. Contrary to traditional thinking, such an environment does not lack control nor respect for the leader. This type of democratic leadership can be usefully extended to the wider issues, such as the spending of the nursing budget. With forethought and good planning this need not slow down the final decision. It may even save time by averting the dissatisfaction which occurs when decisions are made in isolation.

Such procedures may appear to be obvious and well-acknowledged criteria for good management, and yet they are still not freely adopted. It may be that this is due to concentration on management technique, with too little attention to leadership skills. To separate these can only result in a deterioration in nursing care, because the nurses who give this will lose their sense of direction.

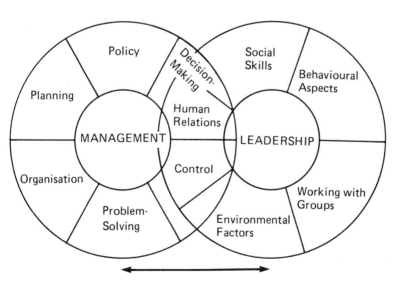

Fig 15.2 The purpose and function of management cannot be separated from leadership

References

1   *Report of the Committee on the Senior Nursing Staff Structure* (Salmon Report). 1966. London: HMSO.
2   White, D. 1980. Some new prospects in management development. *Nursing Focus*, October.
3   Schurr, M. C. 1979. A way of coming together. *Nursing Times*, 30 August. [*Indicates did not appear in original article.]
4   Parkes, K. R. 1980. Occupational stress among student nurses — a comparison of medical and surgical wards. *Nursing Times Occasional Papers*, November, Vol. 76, Nos. 25 and 26.
5   Hawkins, I. R., White, M. G. and Lunn, G. 1980. Stress, smoking and nursing. *Nursing Times*, 1 September ('Over to you' section).
6   Reddin, W. J. 1970. *Management Effectiveness*. Maidenhead: Mc Graw Hill.
7   Ward Sister training. Report of a discourse on a joint training project, Whipp's Cross Hospital and Guy's Hospital. *Nursing Times*, 8 January.
8   *Report of the Royal Commission on the National Health Service* (Merrison Report). 1979. London: HMSO, Cmnd 7615.
9   Crow, R. 1981. *Standards of Nursing Care*. London: Rcn.

16

Professional Reality

To be creative, means ultimately to have the power to receive. In humility we become more than we really are. To give oneself, to receive what is given — this is the breathing of the spirit. This is the foundation of spiritual greatness in man.

Ladislaus Boros

While the discussion continues to decide whether or not nursing deserves professional status, it is often assumed that this is something which depends on function or type of work. In delegating tasks which are considered to be of less importance, professional status is presumed to be enhanced. Nurses have done this for some time, but it would be difficult to argue that this has made any difference to the standing of nurses among other caring professions or the public. If nurses truly believe that it is right to give complete care to patients, satisfying their total needs, this kind of delegation does not make sense.

In reality, professionalism is akin to the quality of the service. It depends on creativity, the search for worthwhile values, and a striving for excellence. For these to be realised, nurses require the humility to recognise and to accept those areas where their contribution can be improved. There has to be professional growth which takes into account increased resources and changing circumstances.

The retention of professional membership is therefore in the hands of nurses themselves. The substance is there, and much has been passed down by inspired and dynamic leaders who have found a place in nursing history. But what of the present? Will the writers of the events of the twentieth century be able to recognise that same striving to meet the challenges of professionalism many of which have been identified in the chapters of this book? There should be no doubt in the reader's mind that the role of the nurse must be a professional one if the needs of society are to be satisfied.

The social contract

Sir Harold Himsworth points out that

> the term 'profession' is a social concept and has no meaning apart
> from Society . . . . It is a tacit social contract inasmuch as there is
> an obligation on the part of the professional individual to use his
> or her 'best endeavours', to meet those particular needs, and there
> is an obligation on the part of society to accord such status,
> authority and privilege as shall be required for the professional
> individual to discharge those obligations.[1]

It is apparent from this statement that to allow standards to fall, or
to restrict in any way the 'best endeavours' endangers the social
contract upon which professional status depends.

The social contract is based on mutual trust. Any contract, if it is
to be binding, is of a two-way nature. It denotes a shared conception
of the objectives, and co-operation to ensure their achievement. It
can be illustrated in this way:

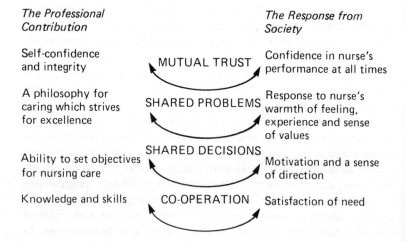

THE SOCIAL CONTRACT

The Professional Contribution		*The Response from Society*
Self-confidence and integrity	MUTUAL TRUST	Confidence in nurse's performance at all times
A philosophy for caring which strives for excellence	SHARED PROBLEMS	Response to nurse's warmth of feeling, experience and sense of values
Ability to set objectives for nursing care	SHARED DECISIONS	Motivation and a sense of direction
Knowledge and skills	CO-OPERATION	Satisfaction of need

Moving towards reality

If progress is to be made toward a more realistic concept of the
nurse's role, a philosophy similar to that outlined on p. 3 must
become a personal code in which individual nurses believe. They
must also believe in themselves, and in their ability to put the

philosophy into practice. In so doing they will find different satisfactions and rewards, as the art of nursing is reinstated and balanced with science and technology. In bringing together these two aspects of nursing a foundation is made for scientific evaluation. It should then be considered sufficiently important to record such problems as making a patient comfortable. Although everyone is unique in their requirements there are common factors which can be applied elsewhere, and from which nurses can learn. For example, the way in which a bed-pan is given to avoid pain, or the placing of pillows. If such nursing incidents are documented, there will emerge a common body of knowledge which has been created by nurses, but is in relation to the *actual* needs of patients, not what nurses think they require.

Matching the need and the job

There are several areas which could usefully be explored, in order to identify the gaps in the delivery of care. For example, at the present time there are many patients who attend their general practitioner over a prolonged period, often with considerable disabilities, and who require help. It may be they only need a knowledgeable and understanding person to listen while they talk about themselves, and matters which do not necessarily require a medical opinion. However, because they do not require actual physical care the nurse does not call, and because they are labelled 'sick', neither does the Health Visitor. Is it time that nurses had the courage to question the efficiency of the present system and consider a new type of health worker in the community? Does the work of the Health Visitor and District Nurse really combine adequately to meet the patient's requirements? It is acknowledged already that there is considerable overlap in the key areas of the educational programme of these grades of staff, and steps are being taken toward shared learning. However, it is questionable whether this goes far enough. It might be possible, for example, to have a foundation course for all nurses wishing to work within the community, including the school nurses, which provided sufficient knowledge to enable them to participate in health education *and* the prevention of illness as they give physical care. It has been known for a nurse to visit the home of a patient suffering from an ulcerated mouth and to give her treatment, but ignore the fact that beside her were packets of biscuits and sponge cakes, whilst oranges remained untouched on the sideboard. The fact that the patient's hands were deformed from arthritis so that she could not manage to peel an orange was also overlooked. However, in criticising such practice it has to be remembered that for many years the teaching of nursing procedures has not always been associated with these broader considerations. Examples of the key areas where at present there is similar teaching in preparing health visitors, district nursing sisters and school nurses are summarised in Table 15.1.

It is not suggested that such an introduction to community nursing could equip all nurses for the highly skilled work at present undertaken by, for instance, the Health Visitor, but unless these aspects of care are combined, the concept of health which has been described in this book will never materialise. Those who want to concentrate on work with families could gain further insight by post-certificate study, perhaps some of this shared with social workers, whereas those who prefer to extend their clinical skills could do this by means of a course provided by the Joint Board of Clinical Studies. These clinical skills might be developed in the field of paediatrics. Far-sighted reports such as that of the Court Committee,[2] which gave firm guidance about the type of nurse the family need to ensure adequate paediatric nursing, have for too long been left on the shelf. If the concept of total care is to be extended into the community, some of the confusion caused by job demarcation must be clarified, so that the family can recognise *their* nurse. The Health Centre has yet to become truly a centre for health, where there is an outward flow of combined expertise, with less emphasis on the jealous protection of traditional roles.

This outflow of expertise is important in yet another context. The clinical nurse specialist has much to offer, especially in situations where the patient needs ready access to advice, and someone who understands the particular problem. There are however dangers in providing specialist services, since they can cause further fragmentation, and the patients may find themselves at the mercy of a variety of helpers all responsible for a part of them. Co-ordination of effort is vital to avoid such problems. The specialist nurses have to be facilitators, people working in the background who guide and teach those responsible for implementing the nursing care plan. They pass on skills, and have an enabling role. They do not take the place of the patient's nurse.

The individual contribution

The ideas expressed above explore just two areas where creative and original thinking is required. To put new ideas to the test is urgent,

Table 15.1 Examples of Common "Key Areas" in the Preparation of Community Nurses

Health Visitor	District Nursing Sister	School Nurse
Observation skills Early detection of ill-health and surveillance of high risk groups.	*Observation Skills and Assessment* Criteria for assessment of total needs of individuals and groups. Normal and disordered body functions. Needs of crisis groups.	*The child as an individual* Physical and cognitive development – recognition of child with special needs.
Social and cultural groups – the development of individuals.	Psychological and social needs of families – the effect of the environment on the individual.	Social development of the child within the family, education, peer and minority groups.
Skills in developing inter-personal relationships.	The dynamics of individual and group relationships – skills in maintenance of effective relationships.	Techniques of interviewing, counselling and communication.
Recognition and identification of need and mobilisation of appropriate resources.	Co-ordination of services – the policies, structure and contribution of other health, social and voluntary services.	The nature, scope and provision of services for the maintenance of health.

Examples extracted from:

1 Batley, N. 1980. Education and training for primary care as seen by a health visitor. *Nursing Times Occasional Papers*, 17 July, Vol. 76, No. 10.
2 Panel of Assessors for District Nurse Training. 1980. Curriculum in District Nursing for State Registered Nurses.
3 Staunton, P. 1977. Guideline for a course in school nursing based on proposals by Council for Education and Training by Health Visitors. *Nursing Times*, 6 November.

but this needs all the skills of introducing change. The process has to be one of smooth and well planned transition. The success of any new venture depends on the amount of co-operation obtained and the inspiration of those who motivate the nursing team toward a more efficient, kindly and broad-minded service. Leaders in nursing must have vision and see the possibilities. Reaching outward and forward has to be an integral part of being a nurse. It is the task of the leaders to release the creativity and motivation is usually strong. This search for fulfilment must be maintained. It is the task of the leaders to release the creativity and the striving among those for whom they provide so that it is channelled usefully and effectively. Only in this way can nurses truly contribute what they have to offer and be satisfied.

Initiative, imagination and courage are perhaps the most needed attributes. There are exciting possibilities if only nurses can break away from the traditional patterns and be prepared to accept the responsibilities as well as the privileges of belonging to a profession. In the discussion document *Towards Standards* prepared by a working committee of the Royal College of Nursing[3] there is a plea for the transfer of authority, accountability, and responsibility to be given to the clinical nurse. However, it is emphasised that this can only be achieved if other disciplines understand and accept this change. Whilst this is true, nurses have to take the initiative and *prove* that they are able to make nursing decisions, and to stand accountable for the quality of care they give. This is the task of the professional, and the means by which professional status can be identified.

If nurses do not grasp this opportunity to demonstrate their unique and specific contribution, others will do this for them, and they will not control their own destiny.

If the thoughts contained in these chapters have helped nurses to clarify their role, the objective will have been achieved. However, the questioning and the searching must go on to ensure progress; remembering that we make our own standards through education, humility and integrity, and that these are the product of learning and living deeply.

References

1   Mackenzie, N. 1971. *The Professional Ethic and the Hospital Service.* Sevenoaks: Hodder and Stoughton.
2   DHSS. 1976. *Fit for the Future: Report of the Committee on Child*

Health Services (Court Report). London: HMSO, Cmnd 6684.

3   Towards Standards, the report of the second year's work of the
    Royal College of Nursing working committee on standards of
    nursing care (England and Wales). 1981. *Nursing Times Report*, 9
    April.

17

What Next?

What could the nurses who have read this book do to find solutions to some of our nursing problems? We have already emphasised in the preface that we do not necessarily have all the answers. However, there are several ideas for rethinking established patterns of nursing practice, which could be a guide for those with the initiative to pursue personal study of their own problems. Sometimes the difficulty is to know where to begin, and the following suggestions may help.

Together with a list of ten questions is a suggested plan of action, and so that the subject can be easily identified, references are included concerning the relevant chapters. Some of the questions will be of particular interest to those working within a specialty, but most can be applied generally.

Question	Suggested Action	Reference
1 Have I a personal philosophy? On what basis is it founded?	Write it down. Examine present practice against what you believe to be right. Do the two comply?	Chapter 2 p. 9
2 Are the patients in my care *really* seen as individuals?	If lack of time is the problem, what can be done about this? Do priorities need sorting? If so, how?	Chapter 1 p. 5 Chapter 3 p. 22
3 How is nursing care delegated in my area of responsibility? Is it always well planned according to assessment of the patient's needs?	Spend time observing what actually happens. Make notes and then discuss with nursing colleagues with a view to action.	Chapter 2 p. 12 Chapter 3 pp. 20—21
4 Do I consider it appropriate to sit and listen to patients? How much time do I give to alleviating their anxieties?	Keep a personal diary for at least two days. Enter your activity every fifteen minutes and mark each period spent listening to patients problems.	Chapter 2 pp. 11—12 Chapter 3 p. 19

Question	Suggested Action	Reference
5 How do I measure nursing standards? Does the nursing team know what is expected of them?	Identify the 'tools' for measurement which you use. Are they adequate? Verify that the nursing team understands what is required.	Chapter 3 p. 17 Chapter 4 p. 35
6 Are there ways in which nurse managers and clinical nurses could work more closely together?	Study the common foundation of the work of these persons on p. 125 with a view to revision of job descriptions	Chapter 15 p. 125
7 Is there an effective working partnership with medical colleagues, and regular opportunity to discuss medical and nursing plans?	Discuss with medical colleagues, and consider the kind of decisions which need to be shared.	Chapter 5 p. 38 Chapter 6 p. 43
8 Am I equipped to deal with the implications of new technology, in order to maintain the balance of nursing care?	Make two lists, one stating the knowledge and skills you have, the other those you consider you need. Find a way of filling the gap.	Chapter 7 p. 55 Chapter 14 p. 110
9 Can teaching and learning be readily and effectively carried out in my area of responsibility?	Ask the nursing team with whom you work what learning opportunities they find. Are they adequate? With their suggestions, make a plan with the help of colleagues in the School of Nursing to provide realistic objectives for learning, to include all the nursing staff.	Chapter 10 p. 82 Chapter 13 p. 111
10 Am I taking an active part in helping others to maintain their personal health and to feel responsible for doing so?	Work out how much time and attention is given to this; and study the information given to patients on discharge regarding their mode of life, and how they can prevent a recurrence of their particular problem.	Chapter 9 p. 74 Chapter 11 p. 94

Index